Sounds Fun

30–50 months

Published 2010 by A&C Black Publishers Limited
36 Soho Square, London, W1D 3QY
www.acblack.com

ISBN 978-1-4081-1466-7

Copyright © A&C Black Publishers Ltd 2010

Written by Sally Featherstone and Su Wall
Design by Trudi Webb
Photographs © Shutterstock, Fotolia and Rebecca Skerne

With thanks to the following schools for their help with the photos:
Valley Children's Centre (Rotherham) and Yarm Preparatory School (Stockton-on-Tees)

Printed in Great Britain by Latimer Trend & Company Limited

A CIP record for this publication is available from the British Library.

To see our full range of titles
Visit www.acblack.com/featherstone

Contents

Introduction

The best environment for communication

It is now well known that communication skills such as eye contact, body language, listening and speaking are at the heart of all learning and development. Children with good communication skills grow up to be confident members of society, who can use their skills to make the most of life inside and out of the education system. We also know that babies and children who, for various reasons, do not develop these skills in early childhood are at risk throughout the rest of their lives. They may fail to make strong relationships with others, they may be less successful in their working lives, and find learning much more difficult.

Such knowledge about language development has resulted in government initiatives such as *Every Child a Talker, Communication Matters* and *Letters and Sounds*, which are intended to support practitioners as they work with babies and children in the ever-increasing range of childcare provision. Some babies and children now spend more time in day - care than they do at home, so the role of practitioners in supporting language development is very important, not just for those children growing up in disadvantaged or lone parent families, but those where both parents work long hours, where the home language is not English, or where the many other pressures of modern life mean that families spend less time together.

While the environment for communication in the early years should ideally replicate the best home situation, there are some factors which practitioners in settings may need to take into account when evaluating their own settings. The impact of radio, television, computers, mobile phones and constant background music has had a significant effect on children's ability to listen, speak and concentrate.

- Practitioners should be aware of these features of home life and restrict the use of television and computers in their setting as much as possible. In fact, many experts say that babies and children should have little or no television or computer exposure until they are three years old. This ideal is perhaps unrealistic in children's home lives, but we should make every effort to counteract this in early years settings.
- Mobile phones, computer games and MP3 players are solitary occupations, often without the involvement of another person, and certainly without the added messages of eye contact, facial expression and body language. Practitioners should bare in mind that the parent who spends much of their time texting or listening to their iPod will not be communicating as much with their child.
- Background music from the radio or television disrupts attention and restricts hearing. Music is a useful tool for practitioners but it should not be used indiscriminately. Keep music at a suitable volume and for particular activities —don't use it as 'aural wallpaper'!

Dummies and pacifiers

Dummies and pacifiers can also be very damaging to language development, particularly when they are used all day. This use restricts the development of speech by reducing the muscular development within the mouth and tongue, as well as endangering the formation of teeth. Practitioners will need to handle this information sensitively when talking to parents, and encourage them to restrict the use of dummies and pacifiers to sleep time or when the child is distressed. Children who crawl, walk or run around with a dummy or feeding cup constantly in their mouth endanger their language development and may endanger their personal safety if they fall. Settings should consider whether to include guidance on dummies, pacifiers and feeding cups in their policies and procedures as well as in their prospectus or guidance to parents.

The role of the Key Person in communication

The role of key person is vital to the success of Sounds Fun activities. Close bonding between key adults and the babies and children in your setting will create a firm foundation for language development. Key members of staff know each child and their family well, and they are in a unique position to nurture language and social development. Their observations will be vital in deciding which activities to plan for the child, and they can create the warm, welcoming and informed link with the child's family.

The key child or key group is at the heart of these activities. They are ideal for key group times, so build them into your daily programme, using individual and small group times for talking, listening, singing and rhymes. Create comfortable places indoors and outside for these key times – settees, armchairs, swing seats, garden benches, bean bags, cushions and rugs are all useful places for language activities where babies and children feel at ease.

Remember that the language you use is crucial to babies' and children's own language development. Use appropriate language whenever you are with children, even if you think they can't hear or are not listening. Children are like sponges and they will soak up your language, whoever you are talking to, and whatever they appear to be doing at the time.

Some tips are:

- If you use 'baby language' such as 'baa-lamb', 'moo-cow' or 'quack-quack' you will restrict children's language development. As a professional you need to help children to learn and use the proper names for animals and objects.
- Don't use slang or 'street language', and discourage others in your setting from using it too. You may need to discuss this as a group and even decide which words are unsuitable. We sometimes use unsuitable words without thinking, and are surprised when children repeat them back to us, or use them in their play.
- Local words or dialect words are part of children's world, but you do need to help them
  to use a range of words, including alternatives to the local ones.

Introduction

Children with additional needs

As Key person you have a responsibility to identify, and if necessary seek help for, children with additional needs. Your setting will have a policy for the support of these children, and if you observe extreme difficulties you should follow the procedures in the policy.

However, some babies and children have developmental delays, which are less severe and can be supported by adapting the activities to make them simpler or less demanding. Other options include choosing activities from an earlier book, or limiting the length of time or the size of the group for the activities you choose. Observation, note-taking and consultation with colleagues and parents will help you to get the right match of activity for each child.

Taking the activities outside

Some children love being outside, are naturally more focused there, and learn best in an outdoor environment, where the sounds, sights, colours and smells are so different from indoors. Outdoor play is now a requirement within the Early Years Foundation Stage, and we have supported this requirement by embedding outdoor activities in all four Sounds Fun books. Each activity in each book has suggestions for taking the idea out of doors, regardless of whether you have a large or small outdoor area.

Some settings have ideal outdoor spaces but of course some of you are providing outdoor experiences in gardens, parks, playgrounds, community spaces or even the balcony of your flat! These are all suitable places for taking 'Talking Time' out of doors and we hope you will adapt the suggestions to fit your own circumstances.

Of course, every setting has its own policies and procedures for outdoor play, and we would strongly advise that you continue to follow these, as every setting is different. However, we would like to add some specific guidance for the 'Talking Time' activities, which we hope will help you to make the most of your outdoor area. Your outdoor area should include spaces for stillness and quiet reflection, away from the busy bikes and ball play. These places could include seats and benches, grassy areas, pop-up tents and other shelters, blankets, mats, cushions, sleeping bags, groundsheets or mattresses. Use these areas for individual or small group times for talking, listening, story telling or singing, and be there in all weathers and during all four seasons. A Place to Talk Outside by Elizabeth Jarman (Featherstone) has some excellent ideas for making sure outdoor spaces are the kind of places young children will develop their language skills.

Involving parents

These books contain a wealth of suggestions for working with parents, and simple ideas for activities parents will be able to do to support their children's learning. The section 'Involving parents' included with each activity suggests things that parents can do at home, things they can bring to show at the setting and other ideas for simple home-based resources.

How will Sounds Fun activities help you?

This series of books is intended to help you help children with sounds, words, talking and reading.

The activities:

- expand the work you are already doing in your own setting to ensure that every child becomes a confident talker and listener – with the best foundations for later speaking, listening, reading and writing;
- support your work with individual children and groups within the Key person process;
- help you in your work with parents, who are children's first and most influential educators;
- provide stimulating and varied activities, carefully matched to the developmental stages in your setting, from babies to children of Reception age, where the activities will be useful support for your phonics sessions.

Which age range are the activities suitable for?

Every activity is presented in the same format to make it easier for you to use within your own planning framework. For ease of use, we have divided the activities into four age ranges, covering the whole of the Early Years Foundation Stage:

- Book 1 covers developmental stages 1 and 2: babies from birth to 20 months (Babies)
- Book 2 covers developmental stages 3 and 4: babies and children from 16 to 36 months (Toddlers)
- Book 3 focuses on development stage 5: children from 30-50 months (Pre-school)
- Book 4 focuses on development stage 6: children from 40 – 60+ months (Reception)

Of course, if you have children whose communication levels are high, you may want to dip into the next book in the series, and if you have children who have individual needs or would benefit from more reinforcement at an earlier stage, you can refer to earlier books.

What's inside each book?

Each book contains 35 activities, each on a double page spread and featuring:

- The focus activity (What you need, what you do and what you say);
- How you could **enhance** the activity by adding more or different resources;
- How you can **extend** the activity for older children or different sized groups;
- Taking the activity **outside** into your garden, a park or other play area;
- Suggestions for **songs, rhymes and stories**;
- **Key vocabulary and gestures** for you to use during the activity;
- Suggestions for **things to look for** as you observe the children during the activity (Look, listen and note);
- How to **use the activity with parents**, either by adapting for home use, or involving parents in your work in the setting.

Some activities will become favourites with the babies and children, and you will return to them again and again in your daily routine, building them into such times as snack, changing and rest times, as well as in the introduction to stories and song sessions.

What's in the box?

This activity is suitable for one or two children

What you need:

A box with a lid e.g. a shoebox is ideal. You could cover it with some wrapping paper

A few familiar objects: a soft toy, a cup, a car, a doll, a hat, a pair of glasses

Enhancing the activity

- Add some toys that make a sound e.g. a bell in a ball, a rattle, a small clock or a timer.
- Collect some objects that link with a current interest or topic.
- To extend language use objects that are all the same colour: a red sock, a red brick, and a red beaker.

Pre-school children love guessing games. This use of familiar objects and any box with a lid will encourage early language, thinking and describing. Play it anywhere with any object that will fit in your box.

What you do

1 Show the empty box to the children and explain that you are going to play a game together. Show them the objects you have collected (not more than three to start with).
2 Now, behind your back or some other screen, put one of your objects in the box (e.g. the teddy). Of course, you need to do this where the children can't see you!
3 Now pass the box round the group, so the children can feel the weight and hear any sound the object makes when they GENTLY shake the box.
4 Ask each child to say what they think is in the box.
5 When everyone has had a guess, let the children take the lid off and see if they were right.
6 Play again with another object.

Extending the challenge

- Put two related items in the box: a cup and saucer, a bowl and spoon, a knife and fork. When the children have named one of the pair, ask them to guess what the other one might be.
- Use some other familiar items, such as a few coins, some Sticklebricks, some pebbles.
- Add some soft items, such as a soft toy, some cotton wool balls, a pair of gloves i.e. things that move about inside the box, and have a weight, but don't make a sound.
- Read *Harry's Box* by Angela McAllister (Bloomsbury) or *The Box* by Martha Lightfoot (Meadowside Children's Books)
  - *Sing a song about the box. Try these words to Twinkle, twinkle little star:*
    Listen hard and you might hear
    What is hiding inside here?
    Does it make a little sound?
    When I move the box around?
    Hold the box and see if you
    Can play the hiding box game too.

Look, listen and note

- *Focus on listening to voices and the object in the box?*
- *Take turns with others?*
- *Name the objects?*
- *Respond to your gestures by actions?*
- *Guess and talk about the objects?*
- *Use phrases such as 'I can hear…'*
- *Stay engaged? How long was his/her attention span?*

Key words and gestures

- Listen (with your hand behind your ear)
- Still (with your hand held up, palm forward)
- Sound
- Guess
- Inside
- Again
- Lid
- Open
- Closed
- Turn

TOP TIP

This activity doesn't need expensive resources – just you, the children, a box, and a few everyday objects to encourage them to listen and talk.

Take it outside

- Have an 'Outside guessing box' and use some familiar natural objects such as a fir cone, shell, stick, leaves or grass.
- Let the children collect some objects to put in the box.
- Take a box on a walk or visit, and play with suitable objects that you have collected.

Involving parents

You could…
- *Have the activity out and show the parents how to do it.*
- *Take photos and display them, so parents can see how you do the activity.*
- *Talk to parents about using everyday materials and objects for this activity.*
- *Display some suitable everyday objects to use for this game, and some empty boxes for parents to help themselves to.*

Let's go for a walk

This activity is suitable for three or more children and is ideal for key group time.

What you need:

No special equipment, just an indoor or outdoor space anywhere.

Focusing on sounds in the world around us is an essential part of developing listening skills. Young children need this listening experience every day. You don't need to spend long, just pop outside, or take time during walks and other outdoor experiences.

Enhancing the activity

- Hang bells, bamboo tubes, wind chimes, old cutlery, strings of shells and other sound makers in your garden or outdoor area.
- Listen for planes and helicopters, and if you hear an interesting sound while the children are playing, such as a fire engine, road mender or ice cream van, stop what you are doing and listen to it together.
- Begin to ask 'Where is the plane?' (Or other sound) and see if the children can point to the source of the sound.

What you do

1 Sit outside with the children, on a chair, cushion, park bench, low wall or a blanket on the grass. You need to be close enough for them to see your face and share the way you listen.
2 Listen together to the sounds you can hear – these may be urban, garden or rural sounds, depending on where you are.
3 Ask the children if they can hear anything, encouraging them to locate the sound and name what or who is making it.
4 Listen carefully yourself, turning your head so you can hear all round, then choose a sound to focus on e.g. an aeroplane, a bird, a car or children playing.
5 Look at the object, and use your gaze to help the children focus on the source of the sound.
6 Talk about the sound you can hear e.g. 'I can hear a car. Look, there it is. Can you see it too?'
7 Don't talk so much that the children can't hear the sounds! Encourage quiet and calm.
8 Now ask one of the children to choose a sound they can hear and talk about it.
9 Don't go on too long, listening is a concentrated activity, little and often is the way to improve listening skills.

Take it outside

- Make sure you go out for listening sessions in every season. There is just as much to hear in the winter or on a rainy day.
- Try a sound session in fog or on a very sunny day – are the environmental sounds different? Is it easier or harder to hear?
- Try sitting with your hands over your eyes and see if this helps with listening.

Look, listen and note

- *Look for children who still find it difficult to sit and concentrate. Give these children very short experiences and plenty of praise.*
- *Note the children who are really getting good at listening. You may want to give them more challenging activities.*
- *Keep a careful note of any child who seems to be having difficulty hearing sounds. They may need a hearing test if this doesn't improve.*

Extending the challenge

- Begin to listen to more subtle sounds, such as the click of a gate, footsteps and raindrops etc.
- Take some photos or find some pictures of the sounds you have heard outside. Take these with you and see if the children can link what they hear with the pictures.
- Sing songs with 'sound effects' such as:

    Round and round the garden
    Listening for sounds
    Can you hear one?
    Listen over here.
    Or
    I hear thunder, I hear thunder
    Hark don't you? Hark don't you?
    Pitter patter raindrops, pitter patter raindrops
    I'm wet through, so are you!
    (To the tune of Frère Jacques)

Key words and gestures

- Listen
- Look
- Can you hear?
- Show me where
- Sound
- Who/what
- Loud/soft
- Sky
- Ground
- Near/far away

TOP TIP
Try lying down on the grass and see what you can hear!

Involving parents

You could...
- *Suggest listening walks as a simple activity, even during a shopping trip.*
- *Remind parents that listening is a key to talking, so children need plenty of experience of the human voice and seeing adult faces in conversations.*
- *Encourage parents to get down to their children's level when speaking to them, and turn front-facing pushchairs and buggies round when they stop for a coffee, a chat or a rest, so the child in the buggy can see the adult's face.*

Tick-tock

Another listening activity for a small group of children.

Enhancing the activity

- Use a different 'sound maker' such as a wind-up musical toy.
- Play this game in different areas of the setting, gradually using a bigger space as children get used to playing and listening.
- Collect some more 'sound makers'.

Involving parents

You could...
- *Show parents how to play this game at home. You could take a series of photos and display these or some of the 'sound making' objects you use.*
- *Ask parents to let you know if their child seems to be suffering from a temporary hearing loss. This will help you to match your expectations to individual needs.*
- *Suggest that parents could remove background noises by occasionally switching off the television.*

It's another way of encouraging children to listen carefully as they search for an object that makes a sound. Collect a wide variety of 'sound makers' for this game, to encourage real listening and fun.

What you do

1 Sit together in a quiet place.
2 Show the children the 'sound maker' and how it works. Pass it round and listen to the sound it makes.
3 Listen to all the other sounds you can hear in the room.
4 Hide the 'sound maker' in the room, and then help the children listen for and then hunt for it.
5 Keep encouraging them to stop and listen – what can they hear?
6 Play again with the same 'sound maker'.

TOP TIP
Try setting the alarm on your mobile phone and asking the children to tell you when it goes off.

Extending the challenge

- Let one of the children hide the 'sound maker'.
- Show the children two 'sound makers' and tell them you will hide just one (remember this is much more difficult!).
- Use a radio or a battery operated CD player with a music CD, set at very low volume.
- Try this rhyme:
    Tick, Tick, Tick, Tick, Tick, Tick, Tick.
    Toast me a sandwich, quick, quick, quick.
    A hamwich, a jamwich, lick, lick, lick.
    Tick, Tick, Tick, Tick, Tick, Tick, Tick

Look, listen and note

- *Note the children who find this game really difficult. They may need practice in smaller groups or one-to-one.*
- *Remember that some children are prone to minor hearing loss when they have a cold and this may affect their ability to join these games.*
- *Children who have good listening skills may enjoy having a game on their own. Watch for these early developers.*
- *Listen to the words and phrases the children use to report what is happening.*

Take it outside

- You will need a louder sound out of doors, but you can still play this game. Try a cooking timer with a long, loud ring.
- Music carries well outside, on a portable CD, where you can adjust the volume to cope with other noises.
- Use your outdoor area for group times as well as for free play. Sometimes go outside when the garden is quiet and play listening games.

Key words and gestures

- Listen
- Hide
- Sound
- Music
- Wind-up
- Key
- Find
- Quiet
- Tiptoe

Behind the screen

This activity is suitable for two or three children from 30-50 months.

What you need:

A selection (not more than three) of 'sound makers', such as timers, wind-up musical toys or a small radio.

An improvised screen such as a big open book or a table easel to hide the sound makers.

Enhancing the activity

- Add another 'sound maker', so you have four.
- Play this game with simple, hand-held musical instruments such as shakers, rattles or bells.
- Play the game in different areas of the setting, so children must listen harder to hear the difference.

Involving parents

You could...
- *Suggest parents play this game by hiding a 'sound maker' inside a cupboard.*
- *Collect some sound making objects for your loan collection or toy library.*

This activity extends 'Tick-tock' by giving children a more complex listening challenge, using the same 'sound makers' and wind-up toys.

What you do

1 Sit somewhere quiet.
2 Show the children the 'sound makers', say the name of each one, and listen to the sound each one makes.
3 Now tell the children you are going to put all the sound makers behind the screen and turn them on one at a time.
4 Put all three sound makers behind the screen and turn one on.
5 Let the children listen and guess which one it is.
6 Play again with either the same sound or a different one, until you have used all three.
7 Give plenty of praise for guessing and naming.

Extending the challenge

- Choose some similar 'sound makers' – maybe two timers that have different 'ticks'.
- Let the children take turns behind the screen and choose a sound maker to turn on.
- Collect some 'sound makers' that make softer sounds.
- Sing the song:
    What is hiding? What is hiding?
    I can't see, I can't see.
    We just have to listen, we just have to listen,
    Carefully, carefully.
    (To I Hear Thunder)

Key words and gestures

- Wait
- Listen
- Choose
- Which one?
- Tick
- Sound
- Loud/soft

Look, listen and note

- Note the children who can hear the object but not discriminate what it is.
- Look for children who can't play the game when they can't see the object. These children need more practice in smaller groups or one-to-one.
- Be aware of health or seasonal differences in some children's listening skills.

Take it outside

- This game is more difficult to play out of doors so you will need noisier items, such as a drum, a cymbal or a CD player.
- Hang a sheet or blanket from a line to make a screen for this and other listening games.
- Make an outdoor listening corner in a quiet part of your garden.

TOP TIP
Use an old mobile phone and alter the ring tones.

Under the blanket

This activity is suitable for two or three children.

What you need:

A piece of fabric such as a blanket or sheet (not too big)

Some familiar objects such as a teddy, a car, a cup, a plastic bucket, a train or a book

A shallow box or tray

This game challenges children to find a hidden toy, remember what it is and then tell someone. Start this game in a friendly, non-threatening way so it's fun for everyone.

What you do

1 Sit together and talk about what the game is about. Tell the children that you are going to hide something under the blanket and they can wriggle under the blanket to find out what it is.
2 Show them the objects you have collected in the tray or box. Help them to name each one.
3 Now hold the edge of the blanket so you can slide the tray and ONE object underneath.
4 Let one of the children wriggle under the blanket to fetch the object and tell you what it is. While they wriggle, you could sing the song below.
5 Repeat the game with another object.

Extending the challenge

- When the children are used to the first version, make the game more difficult by asking them to leave the object under the blanket and try remembering what it is to tell you.
- Use several similar objects – three cars of different colours, three different cups and three farm animals etc.
- Sing:

  We will play the blanket game, the blanket game, the blanket game,
  We will play the blanket game, guess what's underneath.
  (Child's name) has found a yellow car, a yellow car, a yellow car,
  (Child's name) has found a yellow car, who is going next?
  (To the tune of Here we go round the Mulberry Bush)

Enhancing the activity

- If you are working with a bigger group, put several objects under the blanket and let several children fetch one each.
- Try the same game with different fruit, vegetables and small world animals etc.

TOP TIP
Buy some simple sets of plastic picnic tableware, beakers, plates, cups and spoons.

Key words and gestures

- Under
- Hidden
- Find
- Dark
- See
- Hold
- Tell

Look, listen and note

- *Watch for children who are anxious about being in the dark or enclosed spaces. Give these children a less threatening version with a net curtain or voile.*
- *As you make the game more difficult, note those children who find it hard to remember what they can't see.*
- *Note the children who are beginning to use describing words such as colour or size, as well as names to describe the objects.*

Take it outside

- Play this game outside in a pop-up tent. Take the group and the blanket inside the tent.
- Use the game to learn and reinforce the names of natural objects such as cones, leaves, sticks or shells.
- Use a picnic blanket on the grass for a change of physical experience.

Involving parents

You could...
- *Suggest that this is a good game to play under a duvet, or even using small objects under a paper cup!*
- *Encourage parents to use describing words such as colour or size as well as simple names.*
- *Display the sorts of familiar objects you use in your setting for playing games – cups, plates, plastic beakers and spoons etc. This will help them to realise they don't need special equipment to play games at home.*

Susie says...

This is another simple copying activity suitable for a small group of children.

Enhancing the activity

- Cut a hole in the bottom of a box or a bag that fits over your arm. Let the puppet pop out of the top to play the games.
- Let the puppet sing some songs, rhymes and poems line by line, so the children can copy them.
- Let a child control the puppet and lead the game.

Puppets are popular with children of all ages, and they often assume a real character in your setting. You may want to keep a special puppet for 'Talking Time' language games, giving them a special name and their own story.

What you do

1 Introduce the puppet to the children and choose a name for it. Tell the children that the puppet will be coming to group time to help with some games. Remember, you don't have to do funny voices for puppets unless you want to!
2 Now let the puppet show the children how to play the game.
3 Whatever the puppet does, the children must do.
4 Now start by saying 'Susie (or the puppet's name) says clap your hands'. 'Susie says stop.'
5 Make sure all the children understand and can copy the movements.
6 Practise some more simple movements like this before making the game more complicated.

Take it outside

- Puppets can lead outdoor games too. Just bring the 'Talking Time' puppet with you when you go outside or on a walk, so you can do a little listening activity at any time.

Key words and gestures

- Watch
- Puppet
- Copy
- Listen
- Same
- Turn

Extending the challenge

- Let the puppet hide behind a screen, such as a big open book, and give the instructions just by voice.
- Give each child a bean bag, and let the puppet give instructions such as 'Put the bean bag on your head', 'Wave your beanbag in the air' etc.
- Use the puppet to help with naming parts of the body, by saying 'Put your finger on your nose', 'Put your hand on your hair' etc.

Look, listen and note

- *Watch how each child copies the puppet's movements and words.*
- *Note children who find this activity difficult.*
- *Observe and note children who find it difficult to stop when asked.*
- *Look for 'echoing' of the puppet's words.*

Using songs, rhymes and stories

- Sing *Two little dickey birds sitting on a wall.*
- Let the puppet help you to teach the children the song *Put your finger in the air* – find the words to this and lots of other songs by looking on the Internet.

TOP TIP
Using a puppet is a very good way of attracting and sustaining children's attention.

Involving parents

You could...
- *Provide some puppets for the children to use at home. Add some simple tips on using puppets. Some parents are much more adventurous when speaking through a puppet!*
- *Involve parents in the character and story of the 'Talking Time' puppet.*
- *Take some photos of your 'Talking Time' sessions with the puppet and display them where parents and children can see and talk about them.*

Tip-tapping

This activity is suitable for a small group of children.

What you need:

A plastic washing up bowl or bucket

A biscuit tin

A cardboard box

A wicker basket

Some chopsticks or other short sticks for tapping

Enhancing the activity

- Try tapping these objects with different beaters – wooden spoons, metal spoons, washing up brushes, pastry brushes, paintbrushes or plastic fly swatters. Listen for the different sounds.
- Leave the objects in a place where children can play freely with them without disturbing others.

Listening carefully to sounds and spotting the difference between them is a skill that helps speaking and listening. This simple activity will help.

What you do

1 Show the children the different objects you have collected, and make sure they all know the name of each one.
2 Put the objects upside down on the floor in the middle of the space.
3 Now use a chopstick or stick to tap several times on one of the objects. Talk to the children about the sound. Let the children have a go.
4 Now try another object. Does it sound the same? Do they like it better? Is it louder?
5 Let the children experiment with all the different objects and choose which sound they like best.

Take it outside

- Have an outdoor drum band. Buy some buckets and bowls from a bargain shop and set up a band in your garden. Just put the bowls and buckets upside down on the ground and offer the children wooden spoons or mops for beaters.
- Take sticks or beaters outside and listen to the sounds you can make by tapping drainpipes, play equipment, tree trunks, fences and walls etc.
- Hang some old metal saucepans or teapots from a fence and play some outdoor music on them.

Look, listen and note

- *Note children who don't appear to be able to differentiate between sounds.*
- *Observe children who seem unable to play softly or quietly, or children who are obviously distressed by loud noises. These may be signs of hearing problems.*

Key words and gestures

- Play
- Listen
- Copy
- Drum
- Sound
- Different

TOP TIP

Try pound shops and other bargain places for cheap buckets, boxes and bowls.

Extending the challenge

- Have a bowl or box each and play a copying game where one person leads and the others copy.
- Try with two beaters, one in each hand.
- Teach the song *We can play on the big bass drum* and add some verses about playing on a washing up bowl, a big brown box, a biscuit tin etc.
- Put the title *We can play on the big bass drum* into Google for lots of versions to play on the computer.

Involving parents

You could...
- *Encourage parents to have fun with their children, playing tunes on railings at the park, on plastic items or even when children are in the bath.*
- *Suggest ways of making simple home made instruments such as shakers, drums and beaters with household items such as boxes, tins and bottles.*

Sounds and words

An activity suitable for a small group of children.

What you need:

A quiet place

A small drum, box or plastic bowl and a beater

Some familiar objects with names of different lengths. Some suggested objects might be a toy car, a football or a dinosaur. Make sure the objects' names have different lengths (i.e. a different number of syllables).

Linking sounds with the length of words will begin to focus children's listening skills as you concentrate on words of different lengths. Make sure you choose objects with very different sound patterns as this is quite a sophisticated task.

What you do

1 Sit somewhere quiet and comfortable, and look at all the objects. Make sure all the children know what they are called and can say their names.
2 Show the children the drum and beater. Ask a child to choose an object and all say its name together as you beat the rhythm. Repeat this for all the objects, saying the names together as you beat the drum.
3 Now say that you are going to play a guessing game. You will play the beat of the object name and the children can guess which name you are playing by pointing to the object.
4 Make sure you play the rhythm at speaking speed – not too slowly – so the children can recognise the word.
5 Make these sessions short. This is an activity that needs concentration so children may get tired quickly.

Enhancing the activity

- Use your 'Talking Time' puppet to beat the rhythm of the objects or give some of the answers. It often helps if the puppet makes a mistake!
- Collect groups of linked objects such as: pear, apple, banana; pea, carrot, cauliflower; dog, tiger, elephant; car, tractor, fire engine.

Take it outside

- Drumming is great fun out of doors, so provide lots of opportunities for free play with bowls, buckets and other instruments with beaters.
- Make a game of clearing up by beating the drum to the names of the toys and equipment you want the children to collect.
- Play 'I can see...' – a bee, a plane, a butterfly, a raindrop etc. Play two beats and see how many things the children can with two beat names.

Look, listen and note

- *Some children are very good at these games – they are often auditory learners, who learn best by listening. Make sure you give these children quiet places to play and don't worry if they don't always look at you when they are listening.*

- *Watch carefully and don't go on if the children are finding the activity too hard. Try again later, when they are a bit older.*

Key words and gestures

- Listen
- Beat
- Count
- Choose
- Which one?
- Drum
- Beater

TOP TIP

Clapping along to any song will help children develop a sense of rhythm.

Extending the challenge

- Use pictures of objects.
- Try using the patterns of children's names.
- Older children may be able to cope with descriptive words – big boat, little boat, big plane, little car or red fire engine.
- Clapping songs and movement rhymes are very good for rhythmic work and sounds. Try:

  Bumping up and down in my little red wagon.
  Bumping up and down in my little red wagon.
  Bumping up and down in my little red wagon.
  Having so much fun.
  More versions on youtube!

Involving parents

You could...
- *Encourage parents to play clapping games with their children.*
- *Prepare a 'Clapping games sheet' with some familiar songs and rhymes for clapping along to. Leave copies of the sheet where parents can help themselves.*
- *Get some CDs of nursery rhymes to add to your toy library or loan collection.*

Who are you?

This activity is suitable for a small group of children (three or four).

What you need:

A paper plate for each child (and one for you)

A lollipop stick for each child

Felt pens, scissors and coloured paper

Enhancing the activity

- Try cutting out some faces of people and animals from magazines and use these to make masks.
- Provide wool, fur or cotton wool for hair.

Involving parents

You could...
- *Make up some kits for mask making at home, or a set of simple instructions for parents on using the masks.*
- *Take some photos of the children making and using their masks, and display these where parents and children can see and talk about them.*

Making simple masks gives children a new opportunity to make sounds and talk to each other. Paper plates are the easiest first masks, and making them is part of the talking experience.

What you do

1 Sit together at a table and talk about what you are going to do. Look at the resources and let the children choose the sort of mask they want to make.
2 Help them if they need it.
3 Stick the faces on to lollipop sticks or tightly rolled card.
4 Now give the characters names and practise some voices for them.
5 Have some character conversations, holding the masks in front of your faces and making sure the children speak loudly enough for others to hear them.
6 If they decide to just make the animal sounds, that's fine.
7 Remember that some children are scared of masks and may need a gentle introduction to this activity.

Extending the challenge

- Use the animal masks to tell stories or rhymes.
- Add some simple cloaks or tails to make costumes.
- Show the children how to make ears and whiskers etc.

Using songs, rhymes and stories

- Try this version of Twinkle twinkle, little star:

  Make a mask and add a face
  Put some eyes in the right place.
  Now a mouth and wool for hair
  Put the pair of ears just there.
  Now you have a new face too
  Play with me, I've made one too!

Look, listen and note

- *Watch for children who are frightened of masks and work to help them cope.*
- *Listen for the use of different voices. This indicates a good sense of hearing.*
- *Use this opportunity to assess children's fine motor skills and creativity as they work on their masks.*
- *Some children love masks. Watch for children using them in free play and build on this interest.*

Take it outside

- Let the children take their masks outside for free play.
- Have a mask procession round the garden.
- Make up stories out of doors and practise loud voices or animal noises.

TOP TIP
The polystyrene bases from pizzas make good mask bases.

Key words and gestures

- Stick
- Draw
- Make
- Talk
- Voice
- Different
- Face

Body music

This activity is suitable for a group of children

'Body music' is fun to make and easy to do, as it needs no resources apart from hands, legs, tummies, feet and faces. This activity can be done at any time, and in spare moments. As with most 'Sounds Fun' activities, little and often is best.

Enhancing the activity

- Let the children sit facing a friend to make the sounds and movements.
- Use 'body' and 'mouth music' for sound effects in story telling.
- Notice and encourage appropriate use of sounds when children are playing, such as making car or aeroplane noises in play.

What you do

1 Start off sitting together to explore what you can do with your bodies.
2 Sing or say this simple introductory song (to the Twinkle, twinkle tune):
   Look at me, what can I do?
   I can clap my hands, can you?
   I can clap them in the air,
   I can clap them everywhere.
   Look at me, what can I do?
   I can clap my hands, can you?
3 Now adapt the rhyme to other body sounds and actions, such as:
   I can click and flick, can you? (clicking fingers)
   I can slap my knees, can you? (slapping knees gently)
   I can stamp my feet, can you? (stamping while sitting down)
   I can pop my cheeks, can you? (popping with a finger)
   I can hum and buzz, can you? (mouth music)
   I can whisper, Shhh, can you? (whisper the song)
4 Try not to be embarrassed about looking or sounding strange! Body sounds are an important part of making and listening to different sorts of sounds.
5 Short sessions of 'mouth' and 'body music' can happen at any time, such as the start and end of group time.

Key words and gestures

- Listen
- Watch
- Copy
- Hands
- Body
- Mouth
- Tongue
- Legs
- Sound
- Body music

Take it outside

- Take this activity out of doors for some more energetic 'body music' sessions.
- Add sounds to circle games and story times in the garden.
- Make sounds yourself as you play with the children – try to lose your inhibitions!

Look, listen and note

- *Note the control children are developing over the different parts of their bodies.*
- *Look for children who are innovative with body music and sounds, and use these innovations in your sessions.*
- *Note children who have difficulty losing their inhibitions or controlling their enthusiasms!*
- *Listen for differences in the sounds children make.*

Extending the challenge

- Add more body sounds as you think of them, or hear children making them.
- Stand up to make the sounds, and use them in a rhythm as you move around spaces.
- Let children suggest sounds they have invented.
- Try singing along to: *Clap your hands follow me* (A&C Black) or for more ideas look at *Finger Play and Nursery Rhymes* by Sally Featherstone (Baby and Beyond: Featherstone)

Involving parents

You could...
- *Photograph or film the children doing these rhymes and show the parents.*
- *Have a 'Body Music' show where the children share action songs and movement rhymes with their parents and carers.*
- *Make a 'suggestions card' for parents to take home – don't make it complicated – a postcard is a good size for home ideas.*

TOP TIP
Look out for pop groups such as 'Stomp', that use body sounds instead of instruments.

What made that sound?

This activity is suitable for two or three children from 30-50 months.

A quiet place

Three pictures or photos of familiar objects and animals that make sounds e.g. a clock, a dog, a cow, a cat, a baby, a fire engine or a phone.

Enhancing the activity

- You could use objects as well as the pictures to make the game more tactile for younger children.
- Add some different sounds and pictures such as a microwave, a lion, a doorbell and a donkey.
- Let the children test you.

This is another pre-school guessing game, this time, using picture clues as well as sounds to help the children begin to make links between sounds and objects.

What you do

1 Sit together somewhere quiet and look at the cards. Name each object or animal and make the sounds together.
2 Spread the pictures out on the floor so the children can see them the right way up.
3 Now explain that you are going to play a game. You will make a sound and the children should point to the right picture.
4 When you start, look at the right picture as you make the sound. When the children are used to the game, look somewhere else as you make the sound.
5 Add more pictures and sounds when children are ready for them.

Take it outside

- Look for things that make sounds in your garden or outside the fence such as birds, cars, children playing, rain in puddles and other weather sounds. Use these in your game.
- Comment on sounds you hear when you are outside, and praise children who notice them and talk about them too.
- Remember to put plenty of sound makers such as bells and wind chimes in your garden and encourage birds and other wildlife.

Look, listen and note

- *Look at the way the children listen to your sounds and make their own. Can they hear the difference between sounds?*
- *Note any child who has difficulty matching picture and sound, and play the game one-to-one to check.*
- *Watch for turn taking, and those children who just follow others rather than making their own choices.*

Extending the challenge

- Start with more picture cards or objects.
- Take turns to guess the sound.
- Take photos of different objects in your setting.
- Look out for Noisy Jungle, Noisy Animals, Noisy Town (Usborne Books) that have sound buttons to press.
- Sing songs that have sounds in them, such as *Old MacDonald had a farm*.

TOP TIP

Download some clip art from your computer to add to the picture cards.

Key words and gestures

- Sound
- Animal
- Vehicle
- Loud
- Soft
- Look
- Point
- Turn

Involving parents

You could...
- Encourage parents to use the pictures in magazines and books to involve their child in hearing and making the sounds made by familiar things.
- Show them how to play 'I hear with my little ear a sound like this... I wonder what it is?'

Tape recorder fun

This activity is suitable for one or two children.

What you need:

One or two children

A simple, children's tape recorder, Dictaphone or hand held recorder

Using a simple tape recorder to record and listen to their own voices and other sounds is a good experience for young children. Once you have shown them how to work it, the children can do this activity on their own as well as in small groups

What you do

1 Make sure the children know how to use the recorder to record and listen to their own and others' voices. You could record yourself first, so they know what to expect.
2 Now talk about what they would like to record. They could sing, say a rhyme, tell a story or just say their name.
3 Help them to take turns recording their own or each other's voices and playing them back. Some children will never have heard their own voice, so they may need several turns at the activity to get used to what they sound like.

Enhancing the activity

- Try 'Talking Tins', talking photo frames (available from tts-group.co.uk)
- Talking Point items (also from tts-group. co.uk) are useful for prompts, challenges and for interactive displays.
- Record sounds and songs in role-play areas and story corners.

TOP TIP

Encourage children to teach their friends how to use the tape recorder.

Extending the challenge

- Let the children record their own stories to offer in the story corner, with or without headphones.
- Record some favourite stories (or buy some story tapes for your listening corner) and leave them with the storybook for independent listening.
- Record some stories in different languages.
- There are hundreds of CDs and tapes of songs and stories. Collect some of these for your listening corner and occasionally use them in 'Talking Time'.
- Find some recordings of songs and rhymes in other languages.
- Offer CDs and tapes for creative work, role-play and dancing.

Look, listen and note

- *Are the children confident in using the equipment to record and play back.*
- *Note the children who can recognise and differentiate between the voices on the tapes.*
- *Do some children find this activity frightening or difficult? They may need more support.*
- *Can they listen to and concentrate on a favourite story on tape?*
- *Which children choose to listen to and use tape and CD players in free choice time?*

Key words and gestures

- Record
- Play back
- Friend
- Voice
- Different
- Listen
- Story
- Rhyme
- Music

Take it outside

- Use tape recorders and Dictaphones out of doors to record sounds, songs and voices. Play these back at group times and see if children can recognise the voices.
- Use taped sounds to enhance outdoor activities and to extend role-play.
- Get some 'ambient music' – waves, natural sounds, bird song etc to add to outdoor experiences. Don't play it too loud!

Involving parents

You could...
- *Have some information about 'Talking photo frames' and albums, so families can record their children talking about family events.*
- *Encourage parents to experiment with the messages on their telephone answering machine.*
- *Offer cheap Dictaphones or simple recording sticks in your toy library or home loan packs. Add some simple ideas for using them.*

Clap with me!

This activity is suitable for a group of children.

What you need:

A portable CD player or tape player

Some suitable CDs or tapes

Enhancing the activity

- Nursery rhymes are good for clapping, so collect a variety of CDs of these.
- You could record the children singing the rhymes, then play them back in this activity.
- This activity is suitable for the beginning of any group time, with groups of any size. Music and clapping will engage most children immediately.

Take it outside

- Take group times outside for a very different experience.
- Clap as you walk on visits, shopping trips or at the park.
- Play 'Clearing up clapping' as you march around the garden picking up toys and putting them away.

Pre-school children love singing and clapping along to familiar tunes. Collect a variety of different sorts and styles of music. Listen to song CDs before using them to make sure the singing is not too fast or too high/low for the children.

What you do

1. Sit together in a group or circle.
2. Show the children the player and ask if anyone knows how to work it.
3. If the children already know, let one or two take turns to help you with the activity.
4. Now say you are going to play 'One, two, three...clap with me'.
5. Practise the 'One, two, three...' routine before you start. The children should wait until after 'three' and listen to the music before they start clapping in time.
6. Choose some suitable music (instrumental or sung), count 'One, two, three...' then switch the music on and clap along with the children.
7. You may want to fade the music out after a minute or two, so you can practise the 'One, two, three...' before starting a different tune from the same tape.

Look, listen and note

- *Note the children who still can't keep their clapping rhythmical. Let these children sit nearer to you and the music.*
- *Watch for children who can really listen and keep up a rhythm as they clap.*
- *Young children often find it difficult to wait for the music to start. Watch for this ability to emerge.*
- *Note the children who can already operate a simple tape or CD player.*

Key words and gestures

- Stop
- Start
- Wait
- Listen
- Rhyme
- Loud
- Soft
- Clap

Extending the challenge

- Try clapping and singing too. This is more difficult and some children will find it very difficult to do both.
- Alter the volume on the player so children have to listen carefully.
- Play 'Stop, start' stopping the player and starting it again during a track.
- Get a copy of *The Happy Hedgehog Band* by Martin Waddell and Jill Barton (Walker) and clap along to the story of a woodland band.
- Add some nursery rhyme books to your book area, collections and single titles. *The Child's Play* series of single nursery rhyme books (lots of titles) with signing and movement suggestions are perfect for this age.

TOP TIP

Clap along to every song or rhyme you sing. This will help speaking, listening and motor skills.

Involving parents

You could...
- *Provide some simple nursery rhyme books and CDs for lending.*
- *Ask parents if they can remember any rhymes from their childhood and encourage them to teach these to their children.*
- *Take photos of the activity for a wall display or photo book.*

Music mat

This activity is suitable for two or three children.

What you need:

A simple sound mat

Enhancing the activity

- Explore the functions of your mat by letting the children experiment. Different mats will have different features.
- Leave the mat for free play in a music or listening corner.

Jump or dance mats for young children are very useful, and children love using them. Choose a very simple one, and avoid those that have numbers or 'learning' voices, as these will limit their use.

What you do

1 Sit together and look at the dance music mat.
2 Ask the children if they know what it is and how it works.
3 When the children understand how to use it, let them take turns to explore what they can do on the mat and the sounds they can make.
4 Use the mat to help the children take turns and listen to each other's music.
5 When they are ready, encourage counting the steps they make.

Take it outside

- Music mats are great outdoor activities and can be used in free play as long as children know how to take care of them.
- Have a musical mat session out of doors for a change.
- Paint some stepping stones on your path or patio so children can practise jumping from one to another.

Using songs, rhymes and stories

- Try singing a chant such as this as the children move on the mat:

  One, two, what can you do?
  Three, four, can you do more?
  Five, six, add some finger clicks,
  Seven, eight, I can't wait,
  Nine, ten, let's go again.

Look, listen and note

- *Look for children who find this activity difficult or challenging.*
- *Note children who are adept at it and really enjoy this sort of game.*
- *Some children will be able to wait for their turn as they watch others, some will not. Adjust the size of the group to allow for individual differences.*
- *Use this activity as an opportunity to record aspects of physical development.*

Extending the challenge

- Encourage the children to vary their movement patterns and point out the connection with the sound patterns they make.
- Try with two children dancing or moving together.
- Have a go yourself and see what the children think of your efforts!

Involving parents

You could...
- *Add a music mat to your toy library or loan collection.*
- *If parents have a music mat that they don't need, they may be prepared to donate it to your setting.*
- *Older brothers and sisters, as well as parents, may be like to demonstrate their skill on a music mat for the children to enjoy!*

Key words and gestures

- Step
- Jump
- Walk
- Dance
- Count
- Turn
- Wait
- Stop

TOP TIP
If you are given second hand electrical equipment, make sure you have it PAT tested before use.

Follow my leader

This activity is suitable for a group of children.

What you need:

A space to move in

A simple instrument such as a small drum or shaker (optional)

An additional adult if possible

Enhancing the activity

- Add a simple instrument, such as a small drum or tambourine and use this for the 'STOP' sound.
- Play the game all round your setting, in and out of all the areas, stopping and starting fairly often to keep the suspense going.

Involving parents

You could...
- *Tell parents about the game and encourage them to play it with their children when they are out on walks.*
- *This is a very good way to get children upstairs and into bed!*
- *Offer some of the picture books for home sharing.*

Pre-school children love parades and 'Follow my leader' games. This musical version will help children to listen and respond to the sounds you are making. You can add an instrument if you like but voice sounds are best to start with.

What you do

1 Collect the children together and tell them about the game. Say that you are going to play 'Follow my leader' and that you are going to be the leader to start with.
2 Now practise some of the sounds you are going to use and that you would like the children to copy as you march around. You could chuff like a train, 'swish' like grass, 'toot' like a hooter, or just say the word to match your actions: 'stamp, stamp' 'jump, jump' 'hop, hop'
3 You also need to explain that you will stop from time to time, and the children should listen for the word 'STOP' and your hand held up.
4 Now stand in a line with the adult at the front and off you go. Don't go too quickly and if possible use extra adults to help the children to follow the leader. Younger children may find it difficult to stay in a line – don't worry, as long as they are listening to the sounds and following the leader.

Look, listen and note

- *Some children find it really difficult to follow in a bigger group. Give them some practice during free play period when you can start the game informally.*
- *Let individual children take a turn at the front, and observe how they manage this responsibility.*
- *Look for children who can march and do an action at the same time.*
- *How do children manage instruments and other resources as they march?*

Using songs, rhymes and stories

- Try these picture books to follow the activity:
  - *Follow My Leader* by Emma Chichester Clark (Picture Lions)
  - *Copy Cat Faces by Deborah Chancellor* (Dorling Kindersley)
  - *The Copy Crocs by David Bedford* (Oxford University Press)
  - *Rainbow Fish Follow the Leader by Marcus Pfister* (Night Sky)

Key words and gestures

- Watch
- Listen
- Copy
- Follow
- Same
- Stop
- Wait

TOP TIP

Make or buy some bracelets of small bells for children to wear on their wrists or ankles as they move.

Take it outside

- The garden is a great place for this activity. Try it with simple flags or ribbons ticks.
- Play the game at the park, with sticks and leaves for flags.
- Make sure you go everywhere out of doors such as under climbing frames, in and out of the shed, up and down the path.

Extending the challenge

- Once children are used to the game, let a child be the leader.
- Give each child a simple shaker to shake as they follow the leader. This gives an added challenge.
- Add 'turn round', 'walk sideways' and other movements each time you start again.

Make and shake

This activity is suitable for one or two children.

What you need:

Empty plastic water or drink bottles (the small size from children's drinks)

Lentils, dried beans, beads or small dry pasta shapes

Silver duct tape

Enhancing the activity

- Paint the bottles with stripes and spots, using paint mixed with white glue to make it stick.
- When everyone has made a shaker, have a shaker band. Add ready-made shakers from catalogues and educational suppliers.
- Push sticks in the neck of the bottle and seal with duct tape to make handles for the shakers.

Making simple instruments is a great way of involving children in listening to and making sounds. Even the youngest children can manage these simple ideas.

What you do

1 Collect the resources and make sure the bottles are washed and dry (or the contents will go mouldy or may even sprout!)
2 Look at the resources with the children and explain that you are going to make some shakers. Ask them how you could do it and welcome any suggestions.
3 Now let each child take a bottle and put some of the small items inside. They can mix them if they like. Let them decide how many to put in.
4 Help them to put their hand over the top of the bottle to try out the sound it makes when shaken gently.
5 When they are happy with the sound of their shaker, help them to put the top on the bottle and seal it with a strip of duct tape.
6 They could name their bottle by making their mark or name on a sticker or computer label.
7 Now practise using the shakers to accompany songs and rhymes.

Extending the challenge

- Collect all sorts of containers for different shapes, sizes and sounds of shakers.
- Use film canisters and other small containers to make small, palm-sized shakers.
- Cut cardboard tubes or lengths of thick bamboo and fill these with seeds or pasta. Seal the ends to make 'rain sticks'.
- Read *Shake Shake Shake* by Andrea Davis Pinkney (Harcourt Children's Books) or *Shake My Sillies Out* by Raffi (Crown Publications)
- Try *Pat-a-cake: Make and shake* by Sue Nicholls (A & C Black) for more instructions on making simple instruments or *The Little Book of Junk Music* (A & C Black) for ideas on making music with young children.

Take it outside

- Make some big shakers for outdoor play by part filling litre plastic bottles with gravel or sand.
- Take your shaker band out of doors.
- Put up plenty of 'sound makers' in trees and bushes and stand near them to play your shakers.

Look, listen and note

- *Use this activity to observe creative and hand control skills.*
- *Note children who have difficulty playing even these simple instruments.*
- *If younger children have difficulty using the shakers, hold their hands gently in yours as you keep the beat.*
- *Watch for children who have a well-developed sense of rhythm and beat or who can sing and play together at this early age.*

Involving parents

You could...
- *Produce a take-home sheet for parents, to help them make simple instruments with their children: shakers and simple drums etc.*
- *Make a display of familiar objects that can be used to make music: saucepans, wooden spoons, biscuit tins, plastic bowls and boxes etc.*
- *Provide some nursery rhyme CDs for borrowing so children can play along on home made instruments and sound makers.*

TOP TIP
Plastic fridge boxes with lids make good drums.

Key words and gestures

- Fill
- Empty
- Bottle
- Beans
- Pasta
- Shake
- Sound

Rhyme time

This activity is suitable for a small group of children.

Enhancing the activity

- Add some small world animals or characters to help the children predict what comes next in the rhyme.
- Use nursery rhyme anthologies to help you make your own nursery rhyme book and keep it nearby to remind you of the range.
- Make your own versions and let the children help. Just remember, for this activity, the rhyme is the important thing!

Early rhymes are very important for tuning children's hearing and they should be part of every day for every child. Use these at 'key group' times, in small group activity time, and at any moment during the day when you have a bit of spare time.

What you do

1 There are hundreds of rhymes to use with young children, and many can be adapted to make new versions as long as you are inventive. Some have movements but as children get older, it's a good idea to add some that don't have movements, so they can begin to really listen to and anticipate the rhymes.

2 Here is a different version of the popular rhyme Miss Polly had a dolly:

   In the zoo is a bear who will growl, growl, growl,
   And in another cage is an owl, owl, owl,
   And down in the pool is a seal, seal, seal,
   Who is clapping his flippers for a meal, meal, meal,
   And over in the caves is a bat, bat, bat,
   Who is sharing his home with a jungle cat.

3 Once you have a collection of simple rhyming verses, say them frequently together so the children learn them and begin to predict the rhymes.

Look, listen and note

- *Look for children who can hear and say rhymes.*
- *Note any suggestions children make when you ask for rhymes.*
- *Observe closely to make sure you see whether children are genuinely making connections with the sounds or just following others.*

Key words and gestures

- Listen
- Rhyme
- Same
- Sound
- Song
- End
- Turn
- Different

Take it outside

- Play simple rhyming games informally outside.
- Add rhyming books to your outdoor book collections and put these in a basket near a blanket or big cushion.

Involving parents

You could...
- *Encourage them to say and sing rhymes with their children.*
- *Offer lots of rhyming texts and CDs.*
- *Make lists of rhyming words and display these on the parents' notice board.*

Extending the challenge

- When the children are familiar with rhymes try these ways of letting them get involved in listening and predicting:
- Pause before the last word and let the children fill the gap.
- Sing the line and whisper the rhyming word.
- Sing one line with them and then let the children sing the next one.
- Rhyming stories quickly become favourites with young children:
  The Gruffalo and *Room on a Broom,* both by Julia Donaldson, are suitable for this age.
  Shoo Fly, Shoo by Brian Moses (Ladybird Rhyming Storybook) *Engines, Engines: An Indian Counting Rhyme* by Lisa Bruce (Bloomsbury)

TOP TIP
Just before sleep is one of the best times to play listening games.

Change around

This activity is suitable for a small group of children.

What you need:

A collection of rhymes

A space to move in

Action rhymes are good for listening and for an early sense of rhyme. The ability to hear rhyme is a key to phonics and learning to read so give young children plenty of practice in hearing and saying rhymes, with or without actions.

Enhancing the activity

- There are hundreds of nursery rhymes – get an anthology and start making your own versions.
- Ask friends and colleagues to help you make up new versions of old rhymes.
- Involve the children in making up new endings to lines in verses.

What you do

1 Sit together in a group and invite the children to suggest a song to sing together.
2 Every time the children suggest a song, try to think of a way to expand, alter or add extra lines to it. Here is an example, using Humpty Dumpty:

Variation 1

Humpty Dumpty sat on a stone,
Humpty Dumpty, all on his own,
Along came a chicken and made a big nest,
And put Humpty Dumpty in there for a rest.

Variation 2

Mary, Mary up on the swing,
Mary, Mary started to sing,
Along came her puppy and started to bark,
So Mary and puppy went home from the park.

Involving parents

You could...
- *Lend copies of rhymes and rhyming books.*
- *Encourage parents to tell you when their children play with sounds and rhymes, even if they are nonsense.*

Look, listen and note

- *Note the children who are beginning to build up a repertoire of their own songs and rhymes.*
- *Notice and praise children who come up with different ideas for songs to sing and help make up new versions.*
- *Watch carefully for children who seem to have no sense of rhythm or rhyme and monitor their progress in these aspects of early literacy.*

Key words and gestures

- Rhyme
- Same
- Listen
- End
- New
- Silly
- Make-up

Extending the challenge

- Help children to make rhyming pairs by having a basket of rhyming items such as bat/cat, van/man, bee/key and pen/hen. Let the children sort them into pairs.
- Make some silly rhyming pairs for familiar words: apple/dapple/papple/capple – it doesn't matter if they are not real words, as long as the rhyme is there.
- Have available Nursery Rhyme books with CDs such as *Pudding and Pie, Ride a Cock-Horse and Oranges and Lemons* and *Round and Round the Garden*, all by Sarah Williams (Oxford)

Take it outside

- The garden is a great place for singing and circle games. Make sure you use the outdoor area regularly for this activity.
- Sometimes, go outside with a CD or tape player and just put on a nursery rhyme tape. You will soon be joined for a singsong.
- Make outdoor versions of nursery rhyme figures and costumes.

TOP TIP

Hang a clipboard up in your setting and use it to jot down rhymes and rhyming pairs when you think of them.

The wheels on the bus

This activity is suitable for a small group of children.

Enhancing the activity

- Try this activity with the following rhymes:
- *Daddy's taking us to the zoo tomorrow* (adding more animals)
- I went to visit a farm one day (more animals)
- *Row, row, row the boat* adding different sorts of vehicles, such as *Drive, drive, drive your car, gently down the street, merrily, merrily merrily merrily, Now who will you meet?*

Adding new lines to existing songs is another way of extending children's rhyming and creative skills, and their enjoyment of familiar songs. This example can easily be transferred to other songs.

What you do

1 Sit together and sing a song. This example is: The wheels on the bus.
   The wheels on the bus go round and round
   Round and round, round and round
   The wheels on the bus go round and round
   All day long.
2 When you have sung this part of the song, add the other verses the children already know, such as:
   The wipers on the bus go swish, swish, swish...
   The lights on the bus go flash, flash, flash...
3 Now add some different verses about animals and people on the bus, such as:
   The dog on the bus goes woof, woof, woof...
   The lion on the bus goes roar, roar, roar...
   The snake on the bus goes hiss, hiss, hiss...
   The giant on the bus goes stamp, stamp, stamp...
   The ghost on the bus goes whoo, whoo, whoo...
   The Dalek on the bus goes exterminate, exterminate, exterminate...

Take it outside

- Play plenty of action games outside, both as organised groups and in free play with the children.
- Sit with children as they play and either join in songs they are singing or sing by yourself – they will soon join in.
- Don't forget to provide a basket of books for young children to read outside.

Using songs, rhymes and stories

- Annie Kluber's series of Baby Board Books (Child's Play) *Row Your Boat, Heads, Shoulders, Knees and Toes* etc are ideal for children of this age to read with you or on their own.

Look, listen and note

- *Watch for use of movements.*
- *Note children who have a real sense of fun with and delight in words.*
- *Listen for the developing ability to hold a tune – many children take a long time to develop this ability.*

Key words and gestures

- Action words and movements
- Listen
- Rhyme
- New
- Funny
- Same
- Sound

Extending the challenge

- Let the children suggest new characters, animals or other alternatives.
- Make a note of the new versions and use these as the starting point.
- Play a rhyming game where you say a word and they say something that rhymes – it doesn't have to be a real word, just a rhyme.

Involving parents

You could...
- *Use photos and DVDs of the children to help parents learn about rhymes and rhyming. Display the photos and play the DVD where parents and children can see them together.*
- *Provide plenty of loan materials that support rhymes and rhyming.*

TOP TIP
Some practitioners carry a small notebook with them for jotting down new ideas before they forget them!

Counting songs

This activity is suitable for a small group of children.

Enhancing the activity

- Add real objects to any song such as five little frogs, five real (or imitation) buns, five snakes etc.
- Use finger puppets. Find sets for counting in catalogues and on the Internet.

Extending the challenge

- Begin to introduce songs that use ten objects or opportunities to count. Always use objects when singing these songs, because many of them involve counting backwards!

Counting songs and rhymes are favourites with practitioners and children. They are also very easy to adapt by using different words or by incorporating puppets, toys or other objects to help children make sense of counting while they sing.

What you do

1 Sit together and tell the children you are going to sing some counting songs. Ask them to suggest the first one, but have some ready in case they can't.
2 These are some favourites:
      Five little speckled frogs
      Five little ducks
      Five eggs and five eggs
      Five currant buns
3 You can add to this list by altering the originals to:
      Five little spotty snakes, lived in a little lake...
      Five little pigs went trotting one day...
      Five pups, and five pups, and that makes ten, running around in the pet shop pen.
      Five birthday cakes in a baker's shop, round and lovely with candles on the top...

Using songs, rhymes and stories

- Make up your own counting songs and rhymes, using small world toys, natural objects or bargain shop items. Here is a template to use:
      Five little children on a plane
      Flying off to sunny Spain
      (Child's name) stayed for another week
      So only four came back again
      Continue until no children come back, and then sing:
      No little children on a plane
      Flying off to sunny Spain
      School starts soon said Mum and Dad
      So all five little children came back again.

Look, listen and note

- *Note the children who really enjoy these songs and can anticipate the rhymes and know which number comes next.*
- *Look for opportunities to involve children who are hesitant by giving them an object or puppet to hold, or involve them as a character in the rhyme or song.*
- *Use the activity as an opportunity to check their knowledge and use f number and object names.*

TOP TIP

Make some song bags with five objects and a short tape of the song or a Talking Tin so children can play them independently.

Take it outside

- Sing these counting songs out of doors by:
  Finding a log for five 'frogs'
  Filling ten litre bottles with sand for Ten Green Bottles
  Drawing a river for the ducks or using blocks to make a plane or bus.

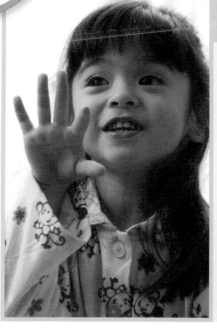

Involving parents

You could...
- *Have some rhyme and song bags with five objects and a song sheet or card, so parents can play the games too.*
- *Encourage parents to focus on numbers from one to five, so the children get plenty of reinforcement before moving on to ten.*
- *Use photos and invite parents to watch the children playing these simple games.*

Key words and gestures

- Count
- Listen
- Sound
- More
- Less
- None
- All

Pop, pop, pop!

This activity is suitable for a small group of children.

What you need:

A space to play the game

A name for this activity ('Silly words' might do)

A follow-on activity at the ready such as a story

Enhancing the activity

- Make the game more active by standing up when you play it, stamping, hopping or slapping in time to the words.
- Use a different starting sound, such as dog, hat, man etc. (short words work best).
- Use your 'Talking Time' puppet or soft toy to 'say' the words for the children to copy.

Making up silly sounds is a very good way of exercising ears and voices, and silly rhymes and jokes are very popular with this age group. This activity has endless variations and can be played at any time with any number of children. It's a good way to start a session such as story time.

What you do

1   Talk together about what you are going to do. Explain that you are going to say a word and then together, you are going to make up some more words that sound the same.
2   Start with 'Pop' and say this three times, clapping as you say the three words.
3   Invite the children to copy you, saying and clapping 'Pop, pop, pop'. Use praise to motivate and keep their attention.
4   Now just change the first letter sound and say this three times (e.g. hop, hop, hop /shop, shop, shop/mop, mop, mop /drop, drop, drop /stop, stop, stop), waiting for the children to copy you. Praise them when they do.
5   Tell them you are going to say some silly words that sound the same, and say one of these three times (e.g. lop, lop, lop /gop, gop, gop /frop, frop, frop /dop, dop, dop /smop, smop, smop – there are hundreds of possibilities).
6   Repeat the new word with them.
7   Continue with the same sound and different rhymes for a few minutes. Don't introduce a new sound in this session.
8   Now say 'That's the end of 'Silly words' for now – we are going to have a story.' This will clearly indicate the end of the activity. Some children will really love 'Silly words', so you need a clear end to this part of the session.
9   When the children are used to the game, you can introduce several sounds and variants in one session, but keep the whole session short and watch for children losing focus.

Extending the challenge

- Start the game and ask a child to suggest the next 'silly word'. Make sure they understand that the word should sound like the one you have just used, but be prepared to praise thought and effort! Let the 'Talking Time' puppet make suggestions and mistakes too.
- Make a list or some cards with starter words and ideas for variations. It's sometimes difficult to think of them when you are busy or under pressure.

Look, listen and note

- *Look and listen for children who get the idea of this game quickly. They will be ready for more and will soon be making up their own versions.*
- *Note children who really are not ready, don't understand and can't join in. These children may need a simpler, less complex game in a one-to-one situation.*
- *Note any spontaneous use of this form of sound game and comment on it to the children. Give praise and use examples from children's own experiments at group times.*

Using songs, rhymes and stories

- Collect nonsense rhymes such as '*Hey diddle, diddle*' and keep them handy to use at group times.
- Tongue twisters are useful ways of using nonsense words or making real words sound like nonsense! Use the Internet to find hundreds to add to your collection.

Try:
- Bubble bobble, bubble bobble, bubble bobble
- Red lorry, yellow lorry, red lorry, yellow lorry, red lorry, yellow lorry
- I scream, you scream, we all scream for ice cream!
- Fuzzy Wuzzy was a bear, Fuzzy Wuzzy had no hair, Fuzzy Wuzzy wasn't fuzzy... was he?

Involving parents

You could...
- *Explain to parents that making up nonsense words is a very good pre-reading activity.*
- *Ask parents for any tongue twisters or nonsense rhymes they remember and make a book or display.*

Take it outside

- Sing silly songs and tongue twisters outside.
- March around playing 'Silly words' follow my leader.
- Encourage children to make up their own words and variations on the words they know.

TOP TIP
A puppet or toy that just appears at 'Talking Time' is a useful prop for all sorts of games.

Key words and gestures

- Sound
- Same
- Different
- Real word
- Silly word
- More
- Times
- Copy
- Think
- Listen

Animal sounds

This activity is suitable for three or four children.

Making animal noises is fun for all children of this age and the louder the sound the better, so collect a range of toy or small world animals, which you can use for all sorts of games including this one. This game helps children to concentrate on sounds and to differentiate between them.

What you do

1 Look at the basket of animals and make sure the children know the names of each and the noises they make.
2 Choose one animal and make its sound.
3 Now pass the animal round the group. Each child makes the sound when they have the animal in their hand, and then passes it on.
4 Put this animal back in the basket, then pass the basket round so each child can choose an animal.
5 Now take turns to hold up the chosen animal and make the sound.
6 Continue the game by doing some of the following:
   - Saying 'Which animal makes this sound…?'
   - Letting the children hide the animals behind their back and taking turns to make the sound for others to guess the animal.
   - Saying 'I wonder who has the animal that makes this sound…'

Look, listen and note

- *Watch carefully for children who just follow others and have difficulty with naming and making noises independently.*
- *Look for turn taking and listening to others.*
- *Be particularly aware of children with EAL and their knowledge of naming words and sounds.*
- *Note children who find it difficult to make the sounds on their own.*

Take it outside

- Play role play games with animal masks, tails and costumes.
- Make the jungle or a farmyard in your garden for noisy play.
- Have some times when children can be really noisy and experiment with managing the volume of their voices, but be aware of children who hate loud noises.

Extending the challenge

- Returning all the animals to the basket and saying 'child's name can you find the animal that makes this sound?'
- Saying 'I'm thinking of an animal that makes this noise...'
- Put all the animals in a bag and let the children have a 'lucky dip' without being able to see the animals.
- Sing I went to visit a Farm One Day
- Read *Noisy Animals* Book by Felicity Brooks (Usborne). For a noisy game *Animal Noises* by Richard Powell (Treehouse) has a spinner which points to different animals. *Animal Noises* by Dawn Apperley (Bloomsbury) and *Big Eyes, Scary Voice* (a story about owls in the park) by Edel Wignell (Tamarind) are also good books for sharing.

Involving parents

You could...
- *Encourage parents to play the game at home.*
- *Provide the words of songs you sing in your setting.*
- *Make sure 'take-home' books include some with sounds as well as words.*

TOP TIP
Get animal masks from party shops.

Key words and gestures

- Animal
- Sound
- Noise
- Roar
- Loud
- Soft
- Scary
- Listen

My name's funny

This activity is suitable for a small group of children.

What you need:

Your 'Talking Time' puppet or soft toy

A place where children can concentrate and really listen

Enhancing the activity

- If you enjoy puppets, have one on each hand and have a 'funny name' conversation between them. Or work with a colleague and a puppet each.
- Add more puppets, soft toys or characters that children know.

Their name is one of the first words children learn to hear and to say. Use this familiarity for some funny games, but be careful not to upset children or offend their sensitivities.

What you do

1 Use the 'Talking Time' character or puppet to introduce the game. It could say 'I know a funny game. It's called 'My name's funny. . . your name's funny'. I'll show you how to play it.'
2 Work with the character and use their name and your name in this way:
    You: 'My name is Miss Brown.'
    The character: 'Miss Brown, Miss Crown, Miss Frown, Miss Down'
    You: 'What's your name?'
    The character: 'My name is Fluffy.'
    You: 'Fluffy, Wuffy, Duffy, Scruffy.'
3 Now choose a confident child and let the character ask them their name, making the same few nonsense names in reply and letting the child have a go back to the character.
4 Continue with another child, until you have all had a turn. Don't force children who don't want to participate.
5 Move on to another talking activity when everyone has had a go.

Take it outside

- Play the game with object names at clearing up time – collect all the trikes, bikes, wikes, smikes or find all the balls, walls, smalls.
- Call children to you by using two or more versions of their name – 'Sam, Ham, I need you here' 'Martin, Startin do you want to play?'

Look, listen and note

- *Note children who are not able to hear the differences between different versions of names. These children may need more practice with simpler games.*
- *Reward the children who can play the game, with smiles and praise, but be aware that some children may find the game difficult.*
- *Make sure the game is not used to tease vulnerable children or hurt anyone's feelings. This is less likely to happen with younger children!*

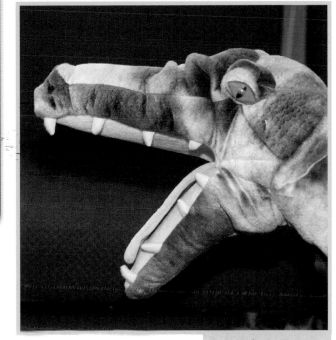

Key words and gestures

- Mouth
- Name
- Sound
- Different
- Silly
- Funny
- Same
- How many

Extending the challenge

- Play the game with a basket of animals such as frog/clog/stog/tog; cow/bow/mow/ tow.
- Share some these books: *Chicky Chicky Chook Chook* a lovely board book by Cathy MacLennan (Boxer Books), *Humpty Dumpty* (Hands-On Songs) by Anthony Lewis (Child's Play), Mr Tig Tog (Lawrence Educational Books) Tip Tip Dig Dig and Toot Toot Beep *Beep* by Emma Garcia (Boxer Books)

TOP TIP

Watching TV can make some children less aware when you need their attention. Always use their name first.

Involving parents

- Share the game with parents, but remind them not to use it to tease their child, just as a game.
- Any use of a child's name in pleasant activities reinforces their knowledge of its sound and their pleasure in hearing parents use it.
- Help parents to use their child's name to attract their attention when they want them to listen.

On the washing line

This activity is suitable for a small group of children.

What you need:

Five or six objects that start with the same sound and two objects that start with a different sound. For this example we have chosen a peg, a penny, a potato, a toy pig, a pen, a panda – and a horse and a big button. Make sure the objects really do start with the same sound, not just the same letter.

A washing line with some transparent plastic bags pegged on.

Enhancing the activity

- Add some pictures of objects as well as objects themselves.
- Collect items that start with common sounds, so you have a bag or box for each of the common sounds in your cupboard. This will save you lots of time!

Beginning to isolate the initial sound in a name is a challenging task, but many children can do this with help by the time they are three. Keep the task simple and collect some objects with names that are easy to say, so there is as much chance as possible of getting it right.

What you do

1. Peg the line up near where you are going to sit.
2. Put all the objects in a basket and sit in a circle somewhere quiet.
3. Sing a simple rhyme as you take each object out of the basket and pass it round. Say:
   'What's this? Yes...
   It's a pig, it's a pig, it's a p-p-pig
   Here he comes, here he comes pig, pig, pig.'
   (as you pass the pig round the circle).
4. When you have taken all the objects out of the basket, including the odd ones out, ask the children if they can find two objects that sound the same. If they find it difficult, pick up one of the 'p' objects and say its name, then ask them if they can find another object with the same sound.
5. When the children have found a matching pair, say p-p-pig, p-p-penny together as they put each one in a bag on the line.
6. Give plenty of praise for listening and matching the sounds.
7. When you only have two objects left in the basket, say their names and talk about why they can't go on the line.

Take it outside

- When you are outside, say the rhyme as you look at familiar objects: 'It's a leaf, it's a leaf, it's a l-l-leaf. Can you find a l-l-leaf like mine?'
- Put up a washing line outside and collect objects that start with the same sound in the same bag.

Look, listen and note

- *Look for children who are already able to hear the similarities and differences between initial sounds.*
- *Be careful to note those children who still have difficulty hearing initial sounds even in a singe word or name of an object.*
- *Note the children who still confuse sounds or are using baby talk.*
- *Listen for speech difficulties such as severe lisps or difficulties with certain sounds.*

Key words and gestures

- Sound
- Listen
- Look
- Same
- Different
- Together
- Choose
- Say

Involving parents

You could...

- *Let parents borrow collections of objects or give them ideas of simple objects such as snake, sock or spoon that they could use for the same sort of sounding rhymes.*
- *Mealtimes are good times for listening – suggest that parents can help by practising sounds in phrases such as 'Would you like a s-s-sausage with your b-b-beans?'*

Extending the challenge

- Once you are sure they can differentiate between the initial sounds, older children could work with a wider range of objects and more than one sound to listen for.
- Have a notebook in your setting with a page for each letter of the alphabet. When you think of new words, add them to save everyone time! Gradually work your way through the initial consonants, giving plenty of repetition of each one.
- Simple tongue twisters are ideal for supporting this activity. Try these or look some up on the Internet:
  - *Red lorry, yellow lorry*
  - *Peter Piper*
  - *Swan swam over the sea*

TOP TIP
Don't go too fast, plenty of practice at the initial level will pay off, particularly with boys, whose hearing develops more slowly.

It's for you!

This activity is suitable for one or two children.

What you need:

A toy telephone each

Playing with toy telephones is a very good listening activity. Having a phone each and phoning each other makes it even more fun.

Enhancing the activity

- As you phone each child, ask them to do something, such as fetch an object or book, hand the phone to another child, call a child from somewhere in the room to talk to you, take a message to another adult etc.
- Use old mobile phones in group times and for role-play. (SAFETY TIP - TAKE THE BATTERIES OUT FIRST)

What you do

1 Let each child take a phone and explore what it does.
2 Now start the activity by 'phoning' a child, saying 'Ring, ring, I'm phoning child's name.'
3 When the child answers have a very short conversation with them, then say goodbye and put down the receiver before phoning another child.
4 When they are ready, let them phone each other, helping them with the turn taking if they need it.
5 This activity is surprisingly attractive for young children and some will play it for hours.
6 Move to the extension activities if they children are ready for more.

Look, listen and note

- *Note the improvement of turn taking in these little conversations.*
- *Some children will not be able to concentrate if they are not the centre of the activity. Make time for one-to-one with these children until they have matured.*
- *Listen for the replies to your questions and instructions, and those children who will just nod or shake their heads.*

Key words and gestures

- Listen
- Speak
- Turn
- Ask
- Say
- Name

Extending the challenge

- Make sure you have phones in all role-play areas and encourage children to phone others and take messages.
- Sometimes use a real phone to call someone or even to order a take-away pizza to share!
- Read Mummy's Big Day Out by Greg Gormley (Bloomsbury). It has a built in telephone and plenty of action!

Take it outside

- Make some telephones from empty tin cans and string or put a small plastic funnel in each end of a length of plastic tubing to create a safe outdoor phone.
- Make or buy a phone box for role-play.

TOP TIP
Offering a child a phone when you are using yours will sometimes stop them pestering when you are trying to listen!

Involving parents

You could...
- *Let parents know how important it is for children to be confident on the telephone, but not be forced to speak to people they don't know very well.*
- *Watching children imitate their parents on the phone is a very good way to learn about them. Get parents to share this information with you when they learn something new about their child.*
- *Have toy phones of all sorts in your toy libraries and loan collections.*

Put it on

This activity is suitable for a small group of children.

What you need:

A large doll or teddy

Some doll's clothes, or baby clothes that fit the doll or teddy

Some other objects such as a cup, a book, a hat and some glasses

Enhancing the activity

- Add more objects such as a doll's chair, doll's bed and bedclothes, flannel, towel and baby hairbrush.
- Put the clothes and other objects in a basket so the child has to find it.

Involving parents

You could...
- *Suggest to parents that baby clothes can be successfully used to dress teddies and dolls, giving children practice for dressing themselves.*
- *Send a message into your community to see if there are any offers of making doll's clothes or bedding for cots and prams.*

This activity supports auditory memory and the skill of following instructions. The first time children play this game the instructions need to be very simple, but they can still be fun.

What you do

1 Sit together, look at all the objects and name each one.
2 Tell the children about the game you are going to play, explaining that you will ask each of them to help the doll/teddy.
3 Now ask the first child to do something – put an item of clothing on the doll, give her a drink or put the hat on her head etc.
4 Make sure everyone gets a turn and ask each time whether the child has done what you asked. Praise the child each time and help them if they need it.
5 When each child has had a turn, decide whether to go on or not. If they have had enough, stop, and play the game again later.
6 If they are ready for more, you could ask them to do something silly, such as 'Put a sock on the doll's hand' or 'Put the cup on the dolls' head.'

Using songs, rhymes and stories

- Sing *Miss Polly had a dolly*.
- Adapt the rhyme *Here we go round the Mulberry Bush* to a doll dressing rhyme – This is the way we dress the doll, dress the doll, dress the doll...
    This is the way we put on her vest, put on her vest, put on her vest... etc.

Key words and gestures

- Doll
- Dress
- Arms
- Legs
- Feet
- Head
- Clothes

Take it outside

- If you have an Empathy doll, get some extra clothes so you can play this game outside.
- Use a doll's pram or buggy to extend the game by asking the children to put the doll in the pram, take her to places in the garden or have a picnic with her.

Look, listen and note

- *Note which children can follow the simple instructions and who can follow more complex ones.*
- *Watch for children who are beginning to be able to follow more complex series of instructions such as 'Find the doll's coat and give it to Michael so he can put it on the doll.'*
- *Some children will watch others to see whether they follow the instructions. These children will be getting a much deeper experience.*

Extending the challenge

- Add a cardboard box and ask the children to put the doll or items of clothing in/on/ under/ behind the box.
- Encourage the children to work together by asking one child to give an item of clothing to another named child to put on the doll.

TOP TIP
Younger children may find it easier to just wrap dolls and teddies in small blankets or sheets.

Finger on your nose

This activity is suitable for one or two children.

What you need:

A space and a group of children

A nursery rhyme book if you need one

Enhancing the activity

- Use beanbags and ask them to put the beanbag on their head, between their knees or on their shoulder.
- Do a more active version that involves children in standing up while following your instructions to put their hand on their foot etc.

Simple instructions are better if there are actions too. This simple activity and some songs to go with it, make a good start to movement instructions involving naming parts of the body.

What you do

1 Start with one or two of these nursery rhymes and encourage the children to do the actions:

   Two little dickey birds
   Tommy thumb
   Wind the bobbin up
   Twinkle, twinkle little star

2 Now tell the children you are going to play a listening game where they must do whatever you say.

3 Children should start with one finger ready to touch parts of their body.

4 Now start to ask them to touch their leg, tummy, knee, ear, eye or nose etc. Praise them for listening and following your instructions.

5 If they can all do these first movements, move on to some more difficult instructions such as eyebrow, shoulder, elbow and ankle etc.

6 If they still want more, let one of the children lead.

Take it outside

- Play the game with big body movements out of doors.
- Play 'Follow your finger' where the children hold a finger in the air and follow it round the garden or play space. Let them do this freely or say 'Up high', 'Down low' etc. to help them vary the way they move.
- Ask the children to put their finger on the climbing frame, the fence, a stone, a leaf or other places in your garden.

Key words and gestures

- Look
- Listen
- Follow
- Carefully
- Next
- Body
- Finger

Look, listen and note

- *Note the children who can follow these simple instructions and those who can't.*
- *Observe the length of time individual children can concentrate on an activity like this.*
- *Watch for restlessness and stop before children get fidgety or bored.*
- *Look for knowledge of simple and more difficult body part names.*

Extending the challenge

- Make the activity more difficult by combining two instructions such as 'Put one hand on your head and the other one on your tummy', 'Put a finger on your ear and a hand on your hair' etc.
- Lots of these songs and rhymes can be found as picture books, which will enable the children to play the games by themselves.

    One finger, one thumb
    Heads, shoulders, knees and toes
    Teddy bear, Teddy bear, touch your toes
    Peter hammers with one hammer
    Put your finger in the air, in the air

Involving parents

You could...
- *Encourage parents to help their children learn the names of body parts when dressing, undressing and bathing.*
- *Add some body part song books to your loan collection.*
- *Make a song sheet with the words for some action songs.*
- *Ask parents if they know any action songs to add to your collection.*

TOP TIP
Pointing and using the index finger is an essential skill for talking and writing.

Can you hear me?

This activity is suitable for a small group of children.

What you need:

A simple tape recorder or Dictaphone

A group of children

A reasonably quiet place

Recording children's voices and playing them back to them is an activity that encourages listening as well as recognising people's voices. The volume control is also a useful listening tool.

What you do

1 Sit in a circle and look at the recorder/Dictaphone. Ask the children if they know what it is, how it works and what it does.
2 When you have all looked at it, let the children experiment with it by singing a song or nursery rhyme together while you record them.
3 Play the recording back to them and show them how the STOP, START, RE-WIND and PAUSE buttons work. Let them take turns stopping, starting, and re-winding themselves.
4 Explore the volume control and play the singing at different volumes.
5 Now ask the children if they would like to record themselves on their own. Don't force them to speak, just encourage them. Let the less confident ones watch and listen until they feel confident enough to join in.
6 Now ask the willing children to say or sing something for the recorder. Make the contributions short, prompt if they need it, and praise all efforts.
7 Now play the recordings back and see if the children can recognise their own and others' voices.

Enhancing the activity

- Get a talking photo frame and put children's photos in alongside their spoken voices.
- Use Talking tins to leave messages and suggestions near activities such as sand and water.
- Try a simple children's karaoke machine.

Extending the challenge

- Let the children record themselves singing or saying rhymes, then see who can guess the voice.
- Get a couple of Dictaphones for use by the children in free play.
- Encourage the children to use a recorder or Dictaphone to record their news and play this back at group times.
- *Little Beaver and the Echo* by Amy MacDonald (Putnam) also has the story on CD
- Many other favourite picture books are now available as CDs. Build a collection for children to listen to in free choice time (with headphones) or at group times.

Look, listen and note

- *Watch for children who are very confident, but be aware of those who are not, and give them the experience in a smaller group or one-to-one.*
- *Observe individual children's listening skills and concentration.*
- *Listen carefully to the recordings. You may be able to hear speech problems that are not so apparent normally.*
- *Note which children can recognise their own or other children's voices.*

Take it outside

- Using tape recorders out of doors means you can make more noise but you also have to listen more carefully.
- Make a sound recording of some of the outdoor sounds of your setting: children playing, bikes, cars going by, birds and a ball bouncing etc. Take some photos of the objects making the sounds and see if children can match the picture to the sound as you play the tape.
- Make a tape when you go for a walk in your community.

Key words and gestures

- Listen
- Loud
- Soft
- Record
- Play back
- Voice
- Who is it?

Involving parents

You could...
- *Encourage parents to experiment with sound recording if they have a recorder at home.*
- *Add some simple story and rhyme CDs to your loan collection.*
- *Suggest that parents may let their child use the recording device on their answering machine to record some messages (parents need to decide whether to use these in public!).*

TOP TIP
Ask parents who speak languages other than English to record some songs and stories for your collection.

Put it there

This activity is suitable for a small group of children.

Enhancing the activity

- Collect several cars of different colours, a few different small world animals, some small world people and some bricks of different shapes and colours. These will enable you to vary the instructions and match the difficulty to individual children.

Positional language is very important, and young children need to learn this by moving objects around in space and by moving themselves. This activity is about moving an object following instructions.

What you do

1 Sit together and look at all the objects in the basket. Make sure all the children know the names of all the objects.
2 Start by asking the children in turn to put an object in the box. Always use the same words and word order: 'Ruby, put the doll in the box' emphasising the position word, and praising them when they succeed.
3 When all the objects are in the box, tip them out and put them back in the basket.
4 Turn the box on its side and use two positional words in and on as you ask the children in turn to put the objects either in or on the box. 'Charlie, put the car in the box.' Or 'Janie put the shell on the box.' Repeat the instruction if they hesitate and praise them for listening and following the instruction.
5 If they want more, introduce 'under' and use one of three instructions as before.

TOP TIP
Another good game for this language is 'I spy with my little eye, something red/blue/round' etc. Give clues like 'It's next to the cupboard' or 'It's under the table'.

Look, listen and note

- *Watch carefully for the way individual children extend their knowledge of these positional words.*
- *Check that children understand the concepts as they tell you where objects are. This will really demonstrate their learning.*
- *Practise this game frequently with children who find it difficult.*

Key words and gestures

- In
- On
- Under
- Through
- Behind
- Between
- In front
- Next to

Involving parents

You could...
- *Show them how to play the game.*
- *Suggest they play the same thing by hiding a teddy or other toy under/on/in/behind their bed.*
- *Challenge them to play a game of tossing their dirty clothes into the washing basket – and shouting 'in' 'out' 'behind' 'over' as appropriate.*

Extending the challenge

- Add more containers so you can give begin to use more complex instructions such as 'Harpreet, put the square brick on top of the red box.'
  Or, even more challenging, 'Mark, put the red car in front of the green box and the blue car under the blanket.'
- Put a blanket on the floor and a box under the blanket, and ask the children to put some objects on, under, in and between the blanket and the box.
- Books to share:
  - *Meeow and the Big Box* by Sebastien Braun (Boxer Books)
  - *Bear and Box* by Cliff Wright (Templar)
  - *Under the Bed* by Paul Bright (Little Tiger Press)

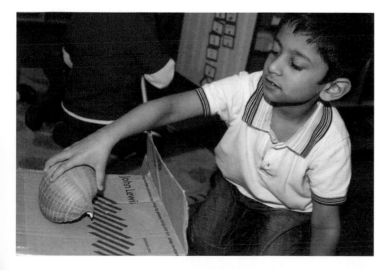

Take it outside

- Play outside with coloured buckets or plastic crates.
- Play a whole body version where you ask children to sit or stand in/on/under/behind different pieces of outdoor play apparatus.
- Hide some small world animals and ask the children to find them and tell you where they were, using positional words.

Guess what?

This activity is suitable for a small group of children.

What you need:

A fabric drawstring bag

Some familiar objects in a basket with a cloth over it or a box with a lid. The objects could include a cup, spoon, small teddy, brick, car, shell, small book, small world animal, a small ball, an apple and a piece of furry fabric

A quiet place to sit

Enhancing the activity

- Add some perfumed or textured objects such as a lemon, a small scented candle or some mint leaves and let the children smell inside the bag as well as feeling.
- If the children find the waiting too long, let them feel inside the bag on the first round.

'Feely' bags are very good for developing language and once you have one, you will find all sorts of uses for it with new vocabulary for shape, object and texture recognition.

What you do

1 Show the children the empty bag and pass it round so they can all feel and explore it.
2 Look at the objects in the basket and make sure the children know what they are all called.
3 Now say you are going to play 'Guess what?'
4 Explain that you are going to put one of the things from the basket in the bag so they can guess what it is.
5 Carefully lift the cover on the box or basket and slide one of the objects into the bag, without the children seeing.
6 Now pass the bag round the group. The first child feels the bag without putting their hands inside and guesses what is in there. Then they pass the bag to the next child who feels and guesses. It doesn't matter if they say the same thing.
7 Continue until everyone has had a guess.
8 Talk about their guesses e.g. 'Some people think it's an apple in the bag, other people think it's a ball. I wonder what it is?'
9 Now pass the bag around again. This time, the children can put their hand inside he bag to feel the texture of the object before they guess again.
10 When they have all had a turn. Let one child tip the object out of the bag. Praise good guessing, not just getting it right!

Extending the challenge

- Collect some similar shaped things, cube shapes, round things, play people of different sorts and small animals and use these for a more difficult game.
- Collect some pieces of fabric, fur fabric, silk, leather and plastic etc. Handle and talk about and describe the fabrics first, then ask the children to describe the texture of the piece you put in the bag.
- You could sing this song together:
    Take the bag and pass it on, pass it on, pass it on,
    Take the bag and pass it on, we're all waiting.
    Can you guess what's in the bag, in the bag, in the bag?
    Can you guess what's in the bag? We're all waiting.
    Now we put our hand inside, hand inside, hand inside,
    Now we put our hand inside, we're all guessing.

Look, listen and note

- *Note which children can wait for a turn and be patient with others.*
- *Listen for god guesses*
- *Watch for children taking their time before guessing*
- *Which children make their own guesses and which ones just repeat the child before them?*

Key words and gestures

- Inside
- Wait
- Turn
- Hand

- Feel
- Carefully
- Outside
- Inside
- Guess

TOP TIP
Handbags and shoes are sometimes sold in useful fabric bags.

Take it outside

- Play the 'Feely bag' game outside with natural objects.
- Comment on things you can feel, but not see, like the wind or sunshine on your skin.

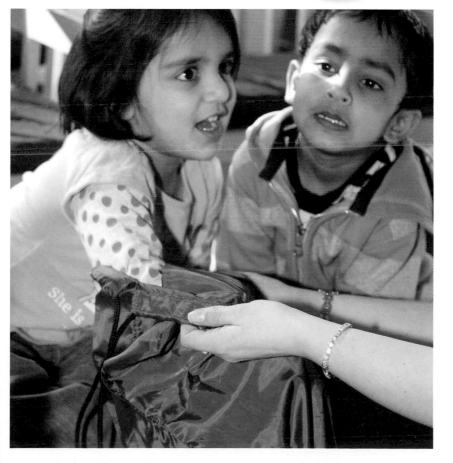

Involving parents

You could...
- *There are lots of 'touch and feel books' available for young children, or you could make your own from fabrics and other tactile surfaces. Put some of these in your loan collection.*
- *Show parents how to play this simple game at home with everyday objects.*

What am I thinking?

This activity is suitable for a small group of children.

What you need:

A tray

About six objects – we chose an apple, a banana, a biscuit, a car, a glove, a sock, a toy cat and a toy bear

Enhancing the activity

- Play the same game but with objects that are all the same colour, all food items or all animals.
- Play the same game but with items of clothing, personal objects such as a toothbrush, hairbrush, comb, flannel and bath duck; or household objects such as a saucepan, kettle, plate, fork, wooden spoon and eggcup.

Another guessing game, this time, based on 'I spy with my little eye'. Make sure you start with a group of objects with obvious distinctions between them.

What you do

1 Sit together in a quiet place and put the tray of object on the floor in the middle.
2 Explore the objects and talk about their names, textures, colours and what each one does or is for.
3 Now say 'Now we are going to play 'What am I thinking about?' I will think about one of these things on the tray and give you a clue. Then you can guess what I am thinking about.'
4 Choose an object and give the children one piece of information, such as the colour, the shape or the texture, e.g. 'I am thinking about something that is smooth'. It's a good idea NOT to look at the object you are thinking about – you could even close your eyes.
5 The children guess and see if they are right.
6 Play again with another object. Once children are used to this game, you could let one of them be the leader.

Take it outside

- Play this game outside with signs of weather, natural objects or toys and games.
- Use a water tray or sand tray and put the objects in the sand or water for a different sort of experience.

TOP TIP
Wrapping paper is very good for making games – buy two sheets, so you can cut one up.

Look, listen and note

- *Watch for children who really can't understand about describing without showing the object. These children will need more practice than some others.*
- *Some children will really love this game. Note who they are and make the game more challenging when they are playing or let them take the lead.*
- *Note the children who are beginning to use and understand function and texture words, such as furry or smooth.*

Extending the challenge

- Begin to play with a wider visual area such as the whole quiet corner, the whole nursery or even things you can't see, but just describe, such as a mum or a star or the wind.
- Take some photos of mixed up animals or other objects and make some 'Spot the object' games. Print two copies, laminate them and cut one into small 'clues' to help the children look for particular objects.

Key words and gestures

- Look
- Listen
- Think
- Words
- Feels
- Smells
- Looks
- Colour

Using songs, rhymes and stories

- *I Spy Little Book*, by Jean Marzollo (Scholastic)
- *Mermaids and Pirates: Let's Play I Spy* by Katie Price (Red Fox)

Involving parents

You could...
- *Make a video or take some photos of this game so parents can play it at home.*
- *Make some very simple 'Spot the object' games for home use.*

What should he do?

This activity is suitable for one or two children.

What you need:

A puppet or soft toy

A quiet place

This is a game for your 'Talking Time' puppet character who has problems for the children to solve. Using a puppet often enables you to talk about real issues without identifying individuals.

Enhancing the activity

- You could use two puppets to have a conversation about a problem they share, such as:
'Penny always wants the wheels in the Lego and so do I!'
Or
'When we are outside, Shafi always want the red bike and won't let me have a go. I really like the red bike, it's the best one.'

What you do

1 Sit together and introduce the puppet. This should be done each time you use it so the children know this activity is special.
2 Now tell the children that the puppet has got a problem that it needs their help with.
3 Here are some starters for you, you'll soon get used to coming up with other ideas. Don't make the problem too complex or stressful, or children may get worried.
4 The puppet could say 'Hello children, I've got a problem today, will you help me?'
   - 'I've lost the key to my money box.'
   - 'My friend doesn't want to play with me.'
   - 'I've broken my mum's best plate.'
   - 'I'm scared of the dark.'
   - 'My baby has scribbled on my best story book.'
   - 'The boys keep running round the garden and pushing me over.'
5 When the puppet has told the children about his/her problem, encourage the children to ask questions and make suggestions about how to solve the problem.
6 Encourage them to take turns and listen to each other.
7 Accept all their suggestions, however strange they may be!
8 When the children have given their suggestions, let the puppet thank them and say that he/she will try some of them. The puppet could say which one they like best but should thank all the children for every suggestion. The aim of this activity is to help children to think.

Take it outside

- When problems occur out of doors, bring the 'Talking Time' puppet outside so the children can talk about the problem immediately.
- Use the 'Talking Time' puppet to explore play problems and difficult situations by getting it to tell stories where the puppet is the character having a problem.

Extending the challenge

- Talk to the children about using the problems they have and encourage them to use the puppet to explain what their problem is.
- Share the following books:
- I Have a Little Problem, said the Bear by Heinz Janisch (North South Books)
- The Problem with Chickens by Bruce McMillan and Gunnella (Walter Lorraine Books)
- Problem Solving by Margaret Martin (Featherstone Education) has lots of ideas for practitioners of how to use problem solving techniques in the Early Years.

Look, listen and note

- *Look for and note children who can empathise with the puppet and its problems.*
- *Listen for the language that children use when making suggestions and whether these suggestions are reasonable.*
- *Note the tone children use when they are offering suggestions and solutions.*

Key words and gestures

- Problem
- Worry
- Listen
- Think
- Choose
- Decide

TOP TIP

Put the 'Talking Time' puppet in a place where it can see the setting as the children play. This will make the activity much more believable.

Involving parents

You could...
- *Encourage parents to adopt a problem solving approach at home by talking things through with their children.*
- *Add some books about coping with worries, such as The Huge Bag of Worries by Virginia Ironside (Hodder Children's Books)*
- *Be ready to discuss parent's worries about their children, especially those in your key group. Be a good listener even though you may be very busy.*

Let's make a story

This activity is suitable for your key group of children.

What you need:

A camera

A scrapbook or home made book with enough pages for a page per child and one for each key adult linked to the group.

Enhancing the activity

- Put the photos on the computer in a simple presentation such as PowerPoint. Add some text and encourage the children to look at the book on screen.
- Use a 'Talking photo frame' or postcard book for the photos, then leave the book on 'play' in the setting so children can see themselves.

This is a good activity for a key group of children. You don't have to do the whole process in one go – you could spread it over several sessions.

What you do

1 Sit with your key group and talk about what you are going to do together. Show them the camera and the book for the photos and talk about making a book about your group.
2 Take a photo of every member of your key group including the adults.
3 Let each group member look at their photo on the camera to make sure they like it! If not, take another one.
4 Print the photos and help each child to stick theirs on a page in the book.
5 If they can, encourage them to use mark making or 'have a go' writing to write their name and any other details they wish to record.
6 If they can't make their own marks, ask them what they would like you to write.
7 Make another copy of all the photos for the children to stick on the cover and add a title to your book.
8 Look at the book together, asking each child to come and help you to read the writing they have done.
9 Put the book in your book corner so children can read it whenever they choose.

Extending the challenge

- Encourage children to take photos of each other using a children's digital camera.
- Make some small copies of the children's photos and add them to your 'making' or 'mark making' table, so the children can make letters and cards for their friends, sticking pictures on the letter or the cover.
- Mount some of the photos on card and make simple puzzles by cutting the pictures into pieces.

Look, listen and note

- *Note whether children are able to recognise themselves and their friends in photos.*
- *Watch for those children who quickly learn how to write or make marks for their own names.*
- *Note any children who really don't like having their photo taken.*

Take it outside

- Make a 'photo wall' by laminating copies of photos or putting them in a Perspex picture frame.
- Hang unbreakable mirrors up in your outdoor areas so children can see themselves and each other.
- Make weatherproof books in plastic display albums for outdoor reading in a cosy shelter or pop-up tent.

TOP TIP
Younger children may like to hold a soft toy or puppet while you take their photo.

Key words and gestures

- Who is this?
- Can you see?
- Eyes, nose, and other body parts
- Colours for hair, skin and eyes
- Smile
- Still
- Move

Using songs, rhymes and stories

- Sing '*Here we go round the Mulberry bush*' or some more personalised versions of nursery rhymes.
- Play '*What shall we do with a girl named 'Katy*' from This Little Puffin: Finger Plays and Nursery Games (Puffin Books)
- Look for some stories about 'me' such as *What I Like about Me* by Miki Sakamoto (Readers Digest) or '*Once There Were Giants*' by Martin Waddell (Walker Books)

Involving parents

You could...
- *Display copies of the photos on the Parents' notice board.*
- *Have some cheap cameras available for children to take home so they can photograph their families.*
- *Encourage children to bring photos into your setting. Discuss these at group times and display them where everyone can see them.*

Doing the washing

This activity is suitable for a small group of children.

What you need:

Doing the Washing by Sarah Garland (Frances Lincoln Children's Books)

A cloth bag, preferably with a drawstring.

Some assorted clothing (children's clothing is easier to peg on a line)

Washing line and pegs

Teapot and mugs

Enhancing the activity

- Make a washing machine together from a big cardboard box. Use sticky tape to close it up, then cut a circle for the door – fixing it at one side with duct tape so it will open and close. The children could use felt pens to draw a control panel and knobs. Use the washing machine to enhance the story next time you read it.

Story sacks make story time more interesting as they capture visual attention. They are particularly useful for those children who find sitting still difficult.

What you do

1 Put the clothing in the bags with the washing line and the pegs.
2 Read the story together without the props.
3 Now look at all the props you have collected.
4 Help the children to hang the washing line up where they can reach it.
5 Now read the story again, and this time, let the children hang the washing on the line at the right page of the story.
6 When all the washing is on the line, sit together and have a cup of tea!

Take it outside

- Washing things in bubbly water is great fun and children love it. Have a car wash or wash all the dolls' clothes and hang them up to dry.
- Use washing lines out of doors for hanging decorative objects such as ribbons, streamers or unwanted CDs. Put the line where there is no risk of children running into the it.
- Tell stories out of doors, not just in the summer – try a story tent, a story in the shed, or grow a living willow or runner bean wigwam. See A Place to Talk Outside by Elizabeth Jarman (Featherstone)

Key words and gestures

- Demonstrate how a peg works, some children may not know!
- Wash
- Dry
- Wind
- Peg
- Basket

Using songs, rhymes and stories

- Sing '*Here we go round the Mulberry bush*' and other action rhymes.
- Adapt some simple nursery rhymes to include familiar activities. This version uses the tune from Twinkle, twinkle little star:
- See the washing going round
    Hear the motor's whirring sound
    Look at all the socks and jeans
    They are getting very clean
    See the washing going round
    Hear the motor's whirring sound

Look, listen and note

- *Use this story to assess how well individual use a pincer grip to peg the washing on the line.*
- *Note any children who don't like joining in with songs and stories. Make some one-to-one time with them.*

TOP TIP
PE shoe bags make great story bags.

Extending the challenge

- Try making your own story bags for favourite stories with lots of action and props.
- Encourage the children to act out stories as you read or tell them.
- Make some simple hats, masks or other props to accompany stories and rhymes.

Involving parents

You could...
- *Start a parents' group and make some story bags for home loan. Start with simple stories where you can easily collect the objects you need.*
- *Ask parents for objects you need for story bags.*
- *Encourage families to make their own story bags or boxes for their children's favourite stories.*

What we like

This activity is suitable for a key group of children.

What you need:

A digital camera

A photo album or scrapbook

Enhancing the activity

- Make some more copies of the photos and laminate them. Stick these near the activities where the children can see them.
- Make more books with other key groups and, at your group time, look at other groups' books.

Pre-school children love photo books, particularly if they are the stars! Digital photography makes it easy to do.

What you do

1. Talk to the children about the things they like doing in your setting and ask them if they would like to make a photo book of the things they like to do.
2. Make a note of what each child likes doing, and over the next day or two, take a photo of them doing their favourite activity.
3. Print the photos.
4. Now sit together and look at all the photos, talking about the activities and who likes doing what.
5. Stick the photos on a book or slip them in an album.
6. Write the child's name under their photo or help them to do it. If you are using a slip sleeve album, you could write the names on stickers.
7. Share the book at group times and keep it in a place where the children can fetch it to look at whenever they like.

Look, listen and note

Do the babies…

- Be sensitive to children who may not like having their photo taken and record this so they are not under stress. Let these children take the photo themselves of what they like so they don't have to be in the photo.
- Note children who can and children who can't choose a favourite activity.

Key words and gestures

- Who
- Favourite
- Best
- Like
- Photo book
- Friend
- Choose
- Keep still!

Take it outside

- Take plenty of photos of the things children like doing outside and make a book of these.
- Let children use simple cameras out of doors to record what they like by taking their own photos. You may be surprised what they decide to photograph!

Using songs, rhymes and stories

- *What I Like!* Poems for the Very Young by Gervase Phinn (Child's Play)
- *What I Like* by Catherine Anholt (Walker books)
- Buy a simple 'Talking Photo' album (http://www.talkingproducts.co.uk) and let each child record a sentence to go with their photo.

Involving parents

You could…
- Encourage parents to share family photos with you by letting their children bring them to your setting.
- Have a 'Photo Corner' on your Parents' Notice board where parents can share their family photos. Respect those parents who are not comfortable with this activity.

Extending the challenge

- Make more photo books and gradually increase the amount of writing under each photo. Add the name for the activity, and then perhaps add a sentence about the child and their favourite activity. Repetition of the same sentence pattern on each page makes it a good early reading experience as you share the book with the group.

TOP TIP

The Tuff Cam from www.tts-group.co.uk and other suppliers is a reliable and easy to use children's camera.

Book list

An expanded compilation of books and stories for supporting early phonics. This list has been compiled to help you in your work with speaking, listening and sounds in nursery and pre-school groups, and includes all the books suggested in Book 3.

Books of activities for speaking and listening

- The Little Book of Bricks and Boxes by Clare Beswick (Featherstone/A & C Black)
- The Little Book of Nursery Rhymes by Sally Featherstone (A & C Black/Featherstone)
- I Spy Little Book by Jean Marzollo (Scholastic)
- Mermaids and Pirates: Let's Play I Spy by Katie Price (Red Fox)
- Problem Solving by Margaret Martin (Featherstone/A & C Black)

Stories and picture books

- Harry's Box by Angela McAllister (Bloomsbury)
- The Box by Martha Lightfoot (Meadowside Children's Books)
- Once There Were Giants by Martin Waddell; (Walker Books)
- The Copy Crocs by David Bedford (OUP)
- Rainbow Fish Follow the Leader by Marcus Pfister (North South Books)
- Bear and Box by Cliff Wright (Templar)
- Under the Bed by Paul Bright (Little Tiger Press)
- I Have a Little Problem, Said the Bear by Heinz Janisch (North South Books)
- The Problem with Chickens by Bruce McMillan and Gunnella (Walter Lorraine Books)
- Spot books by Eric Hill (Warne)
- Meeow and the Big Box by Sebastien Braun (Boxer Books)
- Dear Zoo by Rod Campbell (Macmillan)
- The Happy Hedgehog Band by Martin Waddell (Walker Books)

Rhyming Stories

- Rrring Ring, Tick Tock by Rich Cowley (Firefly)
- Tick Tock Sharks by Elizabeth Mills (Cartwheel)
- This is the Bear; Sarah Hayes (Walker Books)
- This is the Bear in the Scary Night by Sarah Hayes (Walker Books)
- The Gruffalo by Julia Donaldson (Macmillan)
- The Gruffalo's Child; Julia Donaldson (Macmillan)
- Room on a Broom by Julia Donaldson (Macmillan)
- A Squash and a Squeeze by Julia Donaldson (Macmillan)
- The Snail and the Whale by Julia Donaldson (Macmillan)
- Shoo Fly, Shoo (Ladybird Rhyming story books)
- Chicky Chicky Chook Chook by Cathy MacLennan (Boxer Books)
- Mr Tig Tog by Ros Bayley (Lawrence Educational Books)
- Tip Tip Dig Dig, and Toot Toot Beep, Beep by Emma Garcia (Boxer Books)

Some Alphabet Books

- Alligator Alphabet by Stella Blackstone (Barefoot Books)
- Most Amazing Hide-and-Seek Alphabet Book by Robert Crowther (Walker Books)
- The Dinosaur Alphabet Book by Jerry Pallotta (Charlesbridge)
- The Alphabet Book (Dorling Kindersley)
- John Burningham's ABC (Jonathan Cape)
- ABC by Brian Wildsmith (Star Bright Books)
- Picture This by Alison Jay (Templar)

Some Audio Stories and books with CDs

- Pudding and Pie, Ride a Cock-Horse and Oranges and Lemons, Round and Round the Garden: A series of four Nursery Rhyme books with CDs by Sarah Williams (OUP)
- Humpty Dumpty by Anthony Lewis; Child's Play
- Little Beaver and the Echo by Amy MacDonald, (Putnam also has the story on CD)
- The Wheels on the Bus (BBC Audiobooks) (one of a series)
- What I Like! Poems for the Very Young by Gervase Phinn (Child's Play)
- Nursery Rhymes (Book & CD) by Debi Gliori; Dorling Kindersley
- The Puffin Baby and Toddler Treasury (Puffin Books)
- Mother Goose's Nursery Rhymes: and how she came to tell them by Axel Scheffler (MacMIllan)

Non fiction books

- What I Like by Catherine Anholt (Walker books)
- Going for a Walk by Deborah Chancellor (Franklin Watts)
- Going for a Walk Around a School by Sally Hewitt (Franklin Watts)
- Going for a Walk By the River by Sally Hewitt (Franklin Watts)
- Going for a Walk In the Park by Sally Hewitt (Franklin Watts)
- Going for a Walk In the Town by Sally Hewitt (Franklin Watts)
- Going for a Walk By the Seaside by Sally Hewitt (Franklin Watts)
- What I Like about Me by Miki Sakamoto (Readers Digest)
- Copy Cat Faces by Deborah Chancellor (Dorling Kindersley)
- Guess What? Series: Things That Go/Everyday Things/In the Home by Dee Philips (Ticktock Media)
- Guess What I Hear by Liesbet Slegers (Clavis Publishing)

Books about sounds

- Noisy Animals Book; Felicity Brooks (Usborne)
- Animal Noises by Richard Powell (Treehouse)
- Animal Noises by Dawn Apperley (Bloomsbury)
- Big Eyes, Scary Voice by Edel Wignell (Tamarind)
- Mummy's Big Day Out – Fantastic Phones Series by Greg Gormley (Bloomsbury)

Rhyming, rhythm, clapping and beat

- Follow My Leader by Emma Chichester Clark (HarperCollins)
- Shake Shake Shake by Andrea Davis (Pinkney)
- Shake My Sillies Out (Raffi's Songs to Read) by Raffi (Harcourt)
- Row Your Boat, Heads, Shoulders, Knees and Toes and other rhyming board books by Annie Kluber (Child's Play)
- There's a Cow in the Cabbage Patch by Stella Blackstone (Barefoot Books)

Music, Action Songs and Nursery rhymes

- Engines, Engines, an Indian counting rhyme by Lisa Bruce (Bloomsbury)
- Pat a Cake, Make and Shake: Make and Play Your Own Musical Instruments by Sue Nicholls (A & C Black)
- The Ladybird Book of Nursery Rhymes (Ladybird Books)
- This Little Puffin: Finger Plays and Nursery Games by Elizabeth Matterson (Puffin Books)
- Bingo Lingo: Supporting Literacy with Songs and Rhymes by Helen MacGregor (A & C Black)
- Action Songs: Songs to Make You Out of Breath! (HarperCollins)

Featherstone

let's **talk** about

Weather

ISBN 978-1-4081-2668-4

Featherstone

let's **talk** about

Toys

ISBN 978-1-4081-2667-7

Featherstone

let's **talk** about

the Park

ISBN 978-1-4081-2669-1

Featherstone

let's **talk** about

Farms

ISBN 978-1-4081-2666-0

This exciting new series covers the six EYFS areas of learning and development through a variety of age appropriate themes. It fulfils the aims of the Every Child a Talker initiative.

Let's talk about... provides practitioners and children with entertaining, exciting and stimulating language activities that foster and enhance early language learning.